Better Homes and Gardens.

STORAGE PROJECTS
YOU CAN BUILD

BETTER HOMES AND GARDENS BOOKS

Editorial Director: Don Dooley
Executive Editor: Gerald M. Knox
Art Director: Ernest Shelton. Asst. Art Director: Randall Yontz
Production and Copy Editor: David Kirchner
Building and Remodeling Editor: Noel Seney
Building Books Editor: Larry Clayton
Architectural Editor: Stephen Mead
Remodeling and Home Maintenance Editor: David R. Haupert
Building Ideas Editor: Douglas M. Lidster
Remodeling Ideas Editor: Dan Kaercher
Kitchens, Appliances, Home Management Editor: Joan McCloskey
Associate Editor: Kristelle Petersen
Graphic Designers: Harijs Priekulis, Faith Berven, Sheryl Veenschoten

CONTENTS

HOW TO GET THAT EXTRA STORAGE

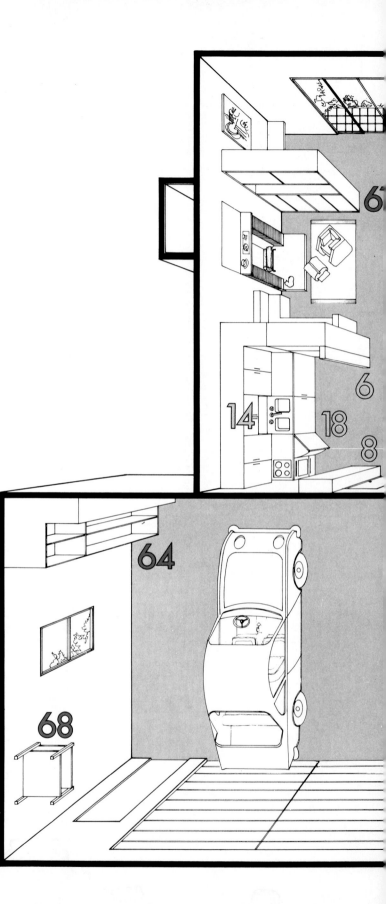

If you have storage problems at your house (and who doesn't), chances are you'll find the solutions in this book. The floor plan shown here will help you decide where you need that extra storage—and where you can put it. The numbers on the plan and below it will steer you to the pages where those projects are shown. Just flip to the appropriate room section and zero in on the particular units you fancy. With each project, you'll find complete step-by-step instructions on how to build it, plus a list of materials to help you easily get a quick cost estimate. What if you lack the know-how? No problem; just turn to page 84 and you'll find all the carpentry and planning help you need. We show you how to make all the standard joints, how to build and install simple drawers, and how to hang cabinet doors with a variety of hinges. There's also handy how-to on all kinds of shelves. Now pick your projects and have at the storage crunch. You have nothing to lose but clutter.

KITCHEN

6 Build a roll-out pantry in a narrow space. **8** Take advantage of wasted walls. **14** Add storage to the backsplash area. **18** Make cabinets fully usable.

BATHS

20 Put dead wall space to work for you. **22** Hang some simple open shelves. **24** Capitalize on all of that area above and around the toilet. **26** Wrap a pair of auxiliary medicine cabinets around one of the unused corners.

LAUNDRY

30 Suspend a convenient shelf/ hanging pole unit from the ceiling. **31** Build a combination clothes hamper/folding table that will make your laundry center complete.

KIDS' BEDROOMS

34 Check floor space for a freestanding unit. **36** Plan wall units that will serve your youngsters' needs. **37** Build roll-around toy storage. **40** Make a closet pay off in extra ways. **41** Combine storage with a built-in bed.

PARENTS' BEDROOMS

47 Use up that space that's going to waste under the bed. **50** Build a combination storage headboard and room divider.

LIVING-DINING-FAMILY ROOMS

52 Plan a whole wall of storage for everything from books to stereos. **55** Make a handsome china cabinet. **56** Border your sofa with interesting shelf units. **59** Put a window wall to work. **61** Use a divider to take advantage of open space.

GARAGE BASEMENT

64 Use a corner of the garage space to stash all that stuff. **67** Make a spot for your tools where there doesn't seem to be room. **68** Suspend a pair of convenient shelves from the open joists above.

SPECIAL PURPOSE

76 Assemble some boxes to make use of an odd space. **81** Construct a ceiling-high, wide open shelf arrangement. **82** Use the dead space in a stud wall. **83** Squeeze out a spot for a bar.

KITCHEN

Any storage crunch looms largest in the kitchen. And, left unsolved, the lack of good storage can cause more inconvenience in the kitchen than in most any other room.

Plus, your kitchen is most vulnerable to ever-growing storage needs. A couple of new appliances, a new set of glassware, or even a change in grocery buying habits can often compound the crunch.

The solution is twofold: make existing space carry a full load, and put unused space to work full time. These projects all do one or the other. So check them carefully to see how you can best accommodate all the things you've stashed away in unhandy places. You'll find ways to make a corner cabinet really usable, suggestions to make an upper cabinet do double duty, tips to utilize the backsplash area between upper and lower cabinets, and a host of adaptable shelving ideas.

All of the projects can be built easily and at low cost. You'll need to adjust some of the sizes to your own requirements in order to make them fit exactly, and our step-by-step directions show you how.

PANTRY IN A SKINNY SPACE

The narrow opening between a refrigerator and a side wall makes a perfect hiding spot for a sliding pantry. This one is just six inches wide, but it has plenty of room for storing canned goods and packages. Open, everything is easy to see. Closed, you'd never guess what's behind the plain face.

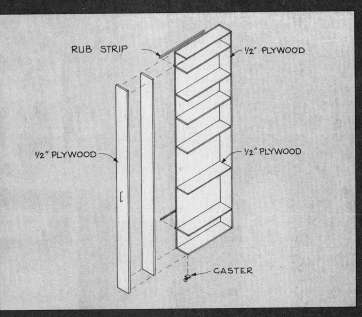

RUB STRIP

½" PLYWOOD

½" PLYWOOD

½" PLYWOOD

CASTER

1 Plan the front-to-back dimension first. The pantry is designed to fit between two stationary ceiling-high uprights; cut these from ¾-inch plywood and nail in place. Cut the surround from ¾-inch plywood, making it deep enough to reach from back wall to front of existing cabinets or side wall. Then cut number of shelves you want to include from ¾-inch plywood.

2 Assemble surround using butt joints. Use white glue and either finishing nails or screws. Install shelves at desired positions using butt joints; again, glue and nail.

3 Cut flush back from ¼-inch plywood. Glue and nail in place.

4 Install heavy-duty drawer glides between unit back and side wall—one at top and one at bottom. Follow directions included in glide package for assembly.

5 Attach one platform caster at front edge of pantry bottom. Lift pantry into place on glides.

6 Cut face to apply to front and finish to match existing cabinets. Glue and nail in place. Attach door pull; fill nail holes.

7 If desired, a flush strip of ½x2 can be attached to shelf edges to prevent cans from falling off shelves.

Materials: For the pantry, you will need 1½ sheets of ¾-inch plywood, one sheet of ¼-inch plywood, two heavy-duty drawer glides, one plate-type caster, nails or screws, door pull, 14 feet of ½x2s for shelf edging strips (optional).

A TOWER OF SPECIAL NICHES

This vertical unit takes up only a couple of square feet of kitchen floor space but provides a wealth of easily accessible open storage. The small butcher block top serves as a mini-counter. You'll want to adjust the sizes of the niches to fit your specific needs exactly.

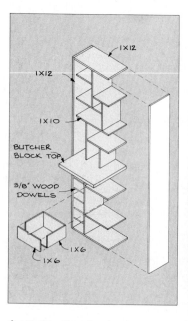

1 Build the basic box with 1x12s—this one is 2 feet wide and 6 feet, 8 inches high. Use butt joints, and glue and nail each corner.

2 Attach the butcher block shelf-counter and the vertical 1x12 below it. You can buy a butcher block to size, or make it yourself out of 1x2 pieces of hardwood. Plan the top 36 inches high.

3 Add the other two 1x12 shelves and wood dowels below. Above, use 1x10s to create the niches. Nail and glue the full-width horizontal 1x10 in place first, then just divide up the rest of the space on a plan-as-you-go basis.

4 Build the drawers from 1x6 boards for the sides and ½-inch plywood for the bottoms. See page 92 for details on the drawers. You can install them with drawer glides (page 92) or cut grooves in the sides and install wood strips to hold them.

5 Slide the unit in place and attach a high shelf as shown here. Or screw small metal angle irons to the top and uprights in inconspicuous places and then drive screws through the angle irons into the wall.

Materials: For the project shown, you'll need 24 lineal feet of 1x12s, 12 lineal feet of 1x10s, 10 feet of ⅜-inch wood dowels, and one 24x18-inch butcher block.

SWING-OUT SHELVES FOR ADDED ROOM

This double-sided shelf unit swings open like another door inside any existing kitchen cabinet. It makes every item reachable—without moving a whole stack. You'll not only appreciate the extra convenience, you'll get a lot more canned goods in the same cabinet.

1 Cut the four 1x6s for the outside frame first. The verticals should be slightly shorter than the opening and the horizontals enough narrower than the opening so the unit will clear when you install it.
2 Remove the existing shelves and cut them back to allow for the 6-inch-deep space you'll need. Then, re-install.
3 Cut dadoes in the center of the 1x6s to receive the ¼-inch hardboard (see page 86) and drill holes for the dowels. Next, assemble the 1x6 frame, hardboard divider, and dowels with nails and glue.
4 Cut and install 1x3 shelves on each side of the unit.
5 Mount the swing-out unit with a piano hinge placed on the same side of the opening as the hinges of the existing door. You may be able to attach the hinge to the back side of the cabinet frame. If not, cut a 2x2 to fit inside the cabinet vertically, screw it in place, and mount the piano hinge on it. Either way, your swing-out shelf will open smoothly.

Materials: For an average-size upper cabinet, you'll need 8 feet of 1x6s, 16 feet of 1x3s, 16 feet of ¼-inch dowels, and a 2x3-foot piece of ¼-inch hardboard.

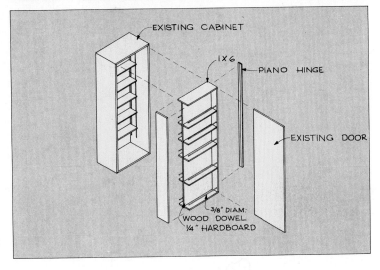

EXISTING CABINET

1X6

PIANO HINGE

EXISTING DOOR

3/8" DIAM.
WOOD DOWEL
¼" HARDBOARD

SHELVES THAT MAKE A WALL COME ALIVE

Once you've installed this storage unit on a kitchen wall, you'll wonder what you ever did without it. You may want to adjust the height of the shelves to keep all of them within easy reach—and with their openness and accessibility, you know they'll be used every day of the year. And, construction couldn't be simpler; it's really just joining boards together.

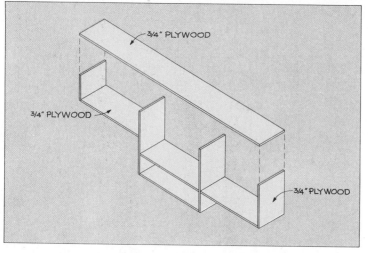

3/4" PLYWOOD

3/4" PLYWOOD

3/4" PLYWOOD

1 Start by cutting the top 1x12 board to fit exactly between the two end walls. Take the time to measure the length from corner to corner and from two corresponding points 12 inches out from the corner. This will indicate any lack of squareness of your walls. Plane off the ends of the 1x12, if necessary, in order to allow for any out-of-square condition.

2 Then plan your divisions and other shelves you want to add. Here, the two vertical dividers were spotted to line up with the ends of the range and refrigerator. You may want to work out a similar design, but be sure to include at least two verticals for an 8-foot-long unit.

3 Cut shelves, dividers, and the two end pieces, and assemble the unit on the floor. Use either butt joints, or cut dadoes (page 86) for the shelves and use rabbet joints (page 86) for the end pieces if you need extra strength.

4 Carefully mark the position on the walls and slide the unit in place. You'll need a helper for this step. Drive three 3-inch screws through each end piece into the wall studs to support the unit.

5 A unit like this is well worth your effort on its own merits, but it also makes a perfect place to install a ductless range hood at the same time. Have an electrician run wires to the spot, and connect and attach the hood to the bottom of the shelf.

Materials: To duplicate this 8-foot-long unit, you'll need 24 lineal feet of 1x12s.

HANG-AND-STORE SYSTEM

Once you've measured how much kitchen wall space is available for this shelf system, you're well on your way. It's easily expandable—or shrinkable—so you can plan it for any wall where you have a few feet of space. And, since the shelves are independent, it's easy to adjust the design to skip roadblocks like an unusually placed electrical outlet.

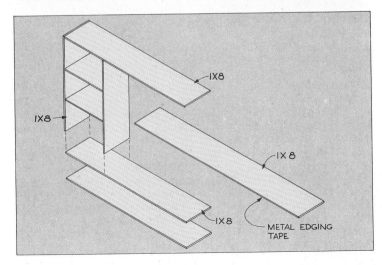

1 Cut the 1x8 boards to the size you've worked out. Here, the longer shelves on the left are 4 feet long; the other shelf is 6 feet long.

2 Assemble the H-shaped box section first, using butt joints. Apply white wood glue and fasten with 6d finishing nails.

3 Then attach the two 4-foot shelves to the top and bottom in the same way.

4 Hang this unit first with metal shelf brackets. You'll need three: two under the lower board and one under the top. Fasten the brackets to the wall with long wood screws into the wall studs. If you can't locate the studs, or if their spacing doesn't work out for you, use either wall anchors or expanding bolts instead. (See the section on page 90, ''Support Systems,'' for help in learning how to locate studs and hanging the shelf brackets.)

5 Hang the separate shelves the same way.

6 Attach paper towel holder and cup hooks to the undersides of the shelves as needed.

7 To duplicate the look of the shelves here, apply metallic tape to the edges of the shelves that will show. Use either stainless steel or aluminum foil tape, press into place, and trim off the excess with a razor blade or sharp knife.

Materials: To duplicate these shelves, you'll need 26 lineal feet of 1x8 pine or fir boards, four pairs of 6-inch shelf brackets, and metallic tape (available in large hardware and craft stores).

CONVENIENCE CENTER

This "worth-all-the-effort" storage/work center serves well in any kitchen. It takes only a little floor space, yet stores a host of your seldom-used items. And you can use it as a mini-office. The swing-up work surface adds to the versatility.

1 Plan to build the center in components, assembling it almost in place. Divide the space you have into thirds for widths of cabinets, and plan the height an inch short of the ceiling. The lower shelves are 16 inches deep; upper depth is 12 inches.
2 Start with the bottom section—cut a back 36 inches high and 1½ inches shorter than your width to allow for the continuous sides.
3 Build a three-sided box for each of the two cabinets; here they are 2 feet wide. On the two interior sides, make a toe space notch. It's also easiest to drill the holes for the shelf supports before you begin assembling. Cut the 16-inch-deep typewriter shelf and the 6-inch-wide apron for the left cabinet. Assemble with butt joints.
4 Next comes the upper part, and again you'll be assembling it without the two long side pieces. Cut the back in the shape of a large T—with the horizontal dimension the same as that for the lower unit. Make the two outside sections 3 feet in the vertical dimension, and the center 4 feet. Then cut the two full-width upper pieces 11¼-inches deep.
5 Build a three-sided box for the open shelves in the middle (don't forget to drill those holes).
6 Cut pieces for the bottoms of the two square cabinets.
7 Assemble the upper components—again using glue and wood screws.
8 Next cut the two long sides that join the components and you're ready to put it all together.
9 Set the lower component

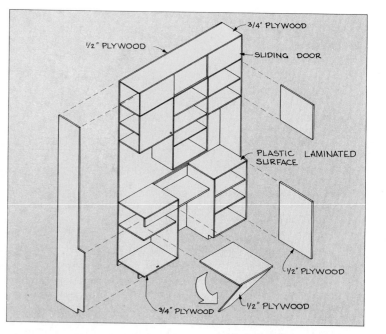

upright, as near to the final spot as you can without blocking access to both ends. Attach the two tall end pieces, again using white glue and wood screws. Then, with assistance, hoist the upper section in place and attach it between the sides, and the toughest part of the job is over. Slide the unit into its permanent spot and drive screws through the back into the wall studs.
10 Cut upper sliding doors from ¼-inch hardboard and install with aluminum or plastic track.
11 Next cut the three hinged doors to fit and attach them.
12 For the swing-up work surface, cut the plywood to fit the door opening and then attach it to the top of the opening with a piano hinge. With a level to check for accuracy, swing the surface out horizontally and measure for the tapered leg. Attach it with hinges, one inch from the ends. The apron above the work surface provides clearance space for the leg when closed.
13 Cut and install the adjustable shelves. As a final touch, install bulletin board material on the wall and cover lower joint with a strip of molding.

Materials: For project as shown, you'll need six sheets of ¾-inch plywood, a 1x6-foot piece of ¼-hardboard, a 3x6-foot piece of bulletin board material, a 6-foot sliding-door track, hinges, pulls, catches, and shelf supports.

UNDER-CABINET CONVENIENCE

Take advantage of the wall space just under the upper cabinets in your kitchen with a unit like this. You may want to divide the interiors of these supplemental bins differently; they're easily tailored to handle whatever you might want to store here. The swing-down doors provide full access, and they close with just a quick flick to cover up the inside.

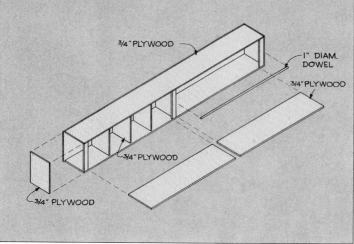

3/4" PLYWOOD

1" DIAM. DOWEL

3/4" PLYWOOD

3/4" PLYWOOD

3/4" PLYWOOD

1 For most kitchens, the best size for this project is 8 inches high and deep. If your existing cabinets are unusually high or low, you may want to adjust the size. And, of course, the length depends on your available space.

2 Cut the top, back, and bottom to a length 1½ inches shorter than the under-cabinet measurement. Then cut the two ends to fit over those pieces. Assemble the box at this point with butt joints.

3 Next cut the four inside dividers to fit the box, with a ¾-inch allowance for the door and trim. Glue and nail these in place.

4 Cut and nail in the 1x2 facing boards at both ends and the center.

5 Attach the assembled box to the wall. You'll need a helper to hold it in place while you drive screws through the back into the wall studs.

6 Cut a 1-inch dowel to fit in one compartment and install it with closet pole hardware.

7 All that's left is the installation of the doors. Cut them to fit and attach them with butt hinges placed at the bottom (see page 93). Buy a short length of furnace chain for the retainers and cut it to the approximate length. Screw one end to the door, then adjust the length and attach the other end to the back of the facing strip.

Materials: For the project as shown, you'll need a half-sheet of ¾-inch plywood, 1½ feet of 1x2s, a 3-foot dowel, four butt hinges, furnace chain, and two pulls and catches.

SLIDE-IN COUNTER ORGANIZER

Here's another way to make the between-cabinet space work full time. Tailor it to neatly hold all the items that are cluttering your counter top. Our directions show you how to plan as you go in order to make the shelves fit your own small appliances, canisters, and whatever else you'd like to get off the counter surface. And—it's very easy to build.

1 Carefully measure the area you want to use and cut the 1x4 frame to fit exactly. Assemble it with ordinary butt joints.

2 Then cut the ¼-inch hardboard back to fit flush and join it to frame with finishing nails and white glue.

3 If the backsplash area has an electrical outlet, now is the time to make a cutout for it. Measure to fix its location and use a saber saw to cut the opening.

4 Now you're ready to start dividing the spaces to accommodate the items you want to store. Cut three or four 1x4s to fit vertically between the top and bottom of the frame. Set the unit up and plan the location of these verticals as needed. When you're set, mark them and remove to apply the glue, then nail in place through the top, bottom, and back.

5 With the verticals in place, measure the length of the horizontal shelves you'll want and cut them to length. Again, you can experiment with their placement, but it's best to put the taller items at the bottom.

6 Nail and glue these shelves in place. This step is easiest if you stand the unit on first one end and then the other. For extra strength, nail through the back also.

7 No installation is necessary. Just gently slide your organizer back into position and it's ready and waiting to go to work for you.

Materials: To duplicate the project as shown here, you'll need a half-sheet of ¼-inch hardboard and 28 lineal feet of 1x4 boards.

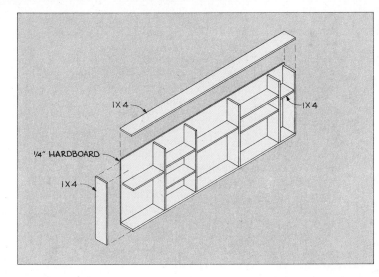

1x4

1x4

1x4

¼" HARDBOARD

ROLL-AROUND THAT HIDES AWAY

This handy roll-around does more than just store things. It takes them right to job. Here it's outfitted to be used whenever there's something to be mixed up for the oven, but you can **easily alter the carrying capacity for other jobs if you like. The roll-around even conceals itself under the counter by re-using one of your existing cabinet fronts.**

1 Choose a base cabinet that was originally installed as a single unit. You'll find the frame will usually pry off quite easily. You'll reattach the frame, door, and drawer front to the new cart.

2 Remove shelves and old cabinet bottom and start measuring. Plan the width of the box you're going to build about 1 inch narrower than the opening. Work out the vertical dimensions to allow for the casters and the canister tops you'll be using.

3 Cut the front and back to size, then cut notches to receive the lower skirt, middle 1x4 brace, and the top shelf. Cut the two solid shelves to the width at the notches, and 3 inches shorter than the existing front-to-back space.

4 Assemble the four larger parts like a big box, then add the skirts, toe board, and the two middle side rails. Use butt joints with glue and finishing nails.

5 Cut the canister-holding top to the full width of the box and nail 1x4s along the bottom edges. Then, with a saber saw, cut the circles to fit your canisters. For the shorter, smaller ones, add a platform underneath. This top shelf can just rest in place, or you can fasten it down permanently if you like.

6 Attach four swiveling plate-type casters to the bottom of the lower shelf.

7 Reattach the old cabinet front with glue and wood screws.

Materials: You'll need one sheet of ¾-inch plywood, 8 feet of 1x4s, and four casters.

MINI-PANTRY ON A DOOR

There's handy storage lurking behind every closed door. Bring it out of hiding with a simple shelf unit like this. Your storage capacity will increase as much as your hard-to-see-and-reach problems will decrease.

1 Build the 1x4 outer frame to get started. Make it as tall as you like, but plan the width about 7 inches narrower than the door itself. This will put the storage unit free of the doorknob and provide the necessary clearance when the door is swung closed. Assemble the outer frame with either butt or rabbet joints.

2 Then start adding the horizontal 1x4 shelves and the 1x2 retaining strips. Work out the spacing according to the size of the items you want to store; there's no need to space them equally.

3 Hang the unit on the back of the door with a ledger strip at the top and bottom (see page 91), or use small shelf brackets placed inconspicuously. Either way, use caution in hanging if the door is the hollow-core type. You can tell by the sound of tapping around the edges versus tapping in the middle. Establish the location of the solid blocking within the door (always around all four sides and sometimes in other locations, too). Then drive screws to support the ledger strips or brackets into blocking and then attach the frame with screws.

Materials: For the project shown, you'll need 22 lineal feet of 1x4s and 12 lineal feet of 1x2s.

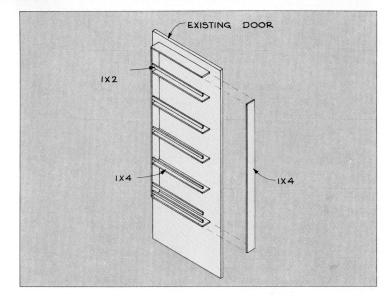

EXISTING DOOR

1X2

1X4

1X4

EASY-REACH LAZY SUSAN SHELVES

Adding semi-circular shelves to the door of an existing corner cabinet turns dead-end space into a handy stash. These swing-out shelves make it easy to store and retrieve dishes, pots and pans, or pantry goods. This project is shown in a base corner cabinet, but will be as effective in an upper cabinet. Just adapt the sizes and add an extra shelf or two.

1 Plan the horizontal dimensions first; the width of the inside cabinet door less 1 inch will equal the radius of the semicircles. Plan the height of the shelves to accommodate your storage needs. Using the modified door measurement, scribe a circle on ¾-inch plywood and cut out with saber saw. Cut the circle exactly in half to make the two shelves.

2 Cut the two back pieces from plywood; the larger one should match the width of the shelves. The shorter one, which provides clearance when the door is closed, should be half that size. Join the two backs and add ledger strips for the shelves.

3 With door backing on flat surface, attach shelves to ledgers with glue and screws. Drill ⅛-inch deep holes for dowels, cut them to fit and glue in place.

4 (Optional) Apply plastic laminate to the shelf surfaces with contact cement. Glue a narrow strip to the top shelf edge and trim off with a plane or file.

5 Cut a 2-inch-wide strip of hardboard to fit around lower shelf. Apply glue, then screw one end to the shelf edge, keep bending and driving screws as you go.

6 Lift shelves and door panel into position and attach to inside of cabinet door with screws and glue. Fill plywood edges with wood putty.

Materials: For a typical base cabinet, you'll need one sheet of ¾-inch plywood, a 4-foot-long strip of ⅛-inch hardboard, 4-foot dowel, and 2x4 foot piece of plastic laminate.

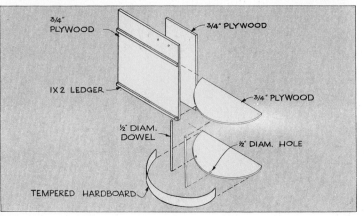

3/4" PLYWOOD   3/4" PLYWOOD

1X2 LEDGER

3/4" PLYWOOD

½" DIAM. DOWEL

½" DIAM. HOLE

TEMPERED HARDBOARD

HANDY STAIR STEP SHELF

This over-the-sink setup puts extra shelves in an unexpected, but very convenient, place. Use this arrangement to span any open space between upper cabinets. It's especially good above a windowless sink, but will serve you well in other spots too. A small fluorescent light fixture mounted under the "stair step" adds extra brightness to the immediate area.

1 Work out the length of the shelves by measuring the spot you have and subtracting 1½ inches to allow for the end pieces. Cut the three horizontal pieces from 1x6 boards.

2 Using butt joints, attach the lower shelf, then the upper shelf, to the horizontal upright, as shown in the drawing. This way, it will fit the two end pieces exactly. Use white glue and either finishing nails or wood screws.

3 Measure and cut the two ends from another piece of 1x6. Fasten them the same way.

4 Install the optional fluorescent light fixture at this point. The simplest method is to screw the fixture to the bottom of the upper shelf and run a cord to a nearby wall outlet. Install an in-line cord switch at an easy-to-reach spot, or have the fixture installed on the wall by a professional. This way, it could be connected to the kitchen wiring so the fixture operates with the others. Either way, the shelf acts as an effective shield for the light.

5 To install, drill two holes in each end piece for wood screws. Carefully slide the unit in place and mark the location of the holes in the sides of the adjacent cabinets. Remove the unit and drill holes; then attach with glue as well as the four screws. Or you can install the unit with a supporting ledger strip attached to the wall (see page 91).

Materials: For a typical over-the-sink unit, you'll need 12 feet of 1x6s, and add the optional light fixture.

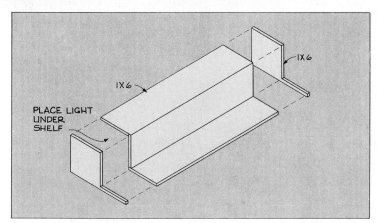

PLACE LIGHT UNDER SHELF

1X6

1X6

BATHROOMS

Just a little attention to storage needs in your bathrooms can mean a big increase in convenience. Because most bathrooms are small to begin with, the storage problems are large. And, bathroom items are the type that really clutter up a room if they aren't stored properly. But even if the problem is tough, the solution can be easier than you think. These out-of-sight storage units will help you get organized. Check all unused wall space as your first step. Then see what projects will best take advantage of the unused areas. Keep in mind that the higher you go, the more storage space you can carve out. Look, too, at your existing medicine cabinet. There's really no need to live with its tiny, overloaded shelves. That cabinet can be replaced or supplemented with one or more of the projects in this chapter. Every one of them is easy to build and uses simple materials, solving your problem with only a minimum of effort. Our directions will speed your work, leaving you more time to finish off your projects with a handsome stain or bright coat of paint to match your color scheme.

This floor-to-ceiling rack/storage unit gets your towels where you need them. Upper level storage takes the place of a regulation medicine cabinet, and clothes pole bars eliminate towel tangles. Use this unit wherever you have dead space, like behind a door. It's only 7½ inches deep.

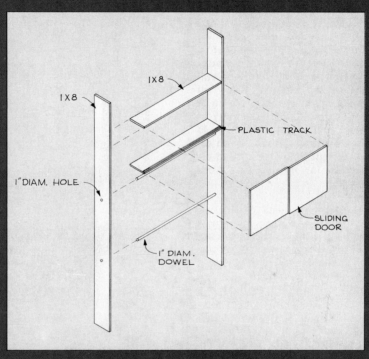

1 Plan the width first (this one is 3 feet); the height should be the same as your floor-to-ceiling measurement. Build the unit on the floor and slip it in place.

2 Cut the 1x8 uprights and notch to go around floor and ceiling moldings if necessary. Drill 1-inch holes to receive clothes poles and cut dadoes in the uprights for the cabinet top and bottom. With dadoed joints, you won't need a back; if you use butt joints, apply a plywood or hardboard back for extra strength.

3 Cut 1x8 cabinet top and 1x8 bottom and join to uprights. Cut and install plastic or aluminum tracks for the sliding doors as shown on page 93. Cut clothes poles, apply glue, and insert.

4 Cut sliding doors from ¼-inch tempered hardboard. Cut finger-holes in doors. Keep the doors about square. If they're very tall, they may bind.

5 To install, position top of uprights and carefully slide the lower part in place. Secure to wall with small angle irons hidden inside the cabinet. Or, with a back, drive screws through it. Slip sliding doors in palce.

Materials: You'll need 14 feet of 1x8s, 6 feet of 1-inch clothes pole, ½ sheet of hardboard, and 3 feet of sliding-door tracks.

QUICK
HANGING
CATCHALL

This hanging shadow box creates storage space in those places where you can't—or would rather not—hammer a nail. Here, the chains are supported by hooks in the wall above the ceramic tile. You could also attach them to a ceiling molding or directly to the ceiling itself. This box is really a drawer that's been divided, but below you'll find direction for making one from scratch.

1 Plan the overall dimensions first; you should keep them small because chains and hooks support the total weight. Cut the verticals from 1x4s and cut dadoes to receive the shelves. Or, you can use butt joints as shown on page 85.

2 Cut the top and bottom of the framework from 1x4s and assemble unit with butt joints. Use white glue and either finishing nails or screws.

3 Cut the shelves from 1x4s and insert in the dadoes. Again, glue and fasten in place.

4 Cut the flush back from ¼-inch hardboard; glue and fasten in place. Fill nail holes and exposed edges with wood putty. Or you could plan an inset back for a neater appearance.

5 Screw decorative hooks into box top and into studs; add lengths of chain to hang.

Materials: For the project shown, you'll need 6 feet 1x4s, ¼ sheet ¼-inch hardboard, 2 decorative screw hooks, and 2 feet of decorative chain.

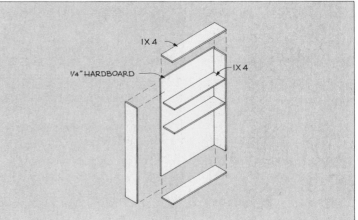

1X 4

¼" HARDBOARD

1X 4

HIS-AND-HERS MEDICINE CHEST

This easy-to-build medicine cabinet lets you handsomely hide all that bathroom clutter. Stock shutters on both sides of the well-lighted mirror conceal the individual, well-organized storage banks. The construction of the medicine chest makes it a simple matter to replace an old one. Just remove it and plan this one large enough to fit over the hole.

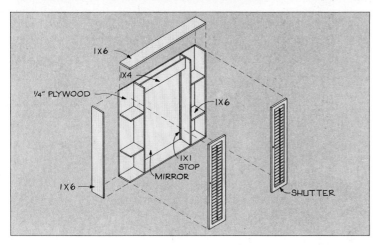

1 Determine the overall dimensions first; work out the height according to the size of the stock louvered shutters you select. The width can be adjusted to whatever space you have on the bathroom wall. Cut the 6-inch-deep framework from ¾-inch plywood. Cut dadoes in the vertical pieces to receive the shelves. Or, choose adjustable shelf strips and install them at this point as shown on page 91. Then assemble frame with butt joints. Use white glue and either finishing nails or screws.

2 Cut the 6-inch-deep shelves from ¼-inch plywood and slip them into the dadoes; again, glue and nail in place.

3 Cut and attach the ¼-inch plywood back. Attaching it flush to the framework is easiest and effective for this unit.

4 Flush-mount 8-inch-wide louvered shutters with butt hinges. Apply knobs and catches.

5 Mount unit on wall by screwing through back into wall studs. Cut sheet acrylic mirror to fit between louvered shutter cabinets and glue in place. Or, install a vertical ½x½ stop at both sides of the mirror to hold it in place. Install fluorescent fixture behind fascia and slip diffuser panel into place.

Materials: For the project shown, you'll need one sheet of ¾-inch plywood, one sheet ¼-inch plywood, 5 feet ½x½s, two 30x8-inch louvered shutters, two door pulls, four butt hinges, two magnetic catches, fluorescent fixture, acrylic diffuser, and an acrylic sheet mirror.

This versatile shelving project opens many practical—and unique—possibilities for your bathroom. Depending on what you stock the shelves with, you can turn your bathroom into anything from a mini-library to a supplemental linen closet. Here it's shown in a compart-mented bathroom, but you can adapt it to any situation. Even if you have space for only the center section, you'll still have a whale of a lot of extra space. Just reduce the length of the 4-foot-wide top piece and make sure the verticals are securely fastened both to it and the walls.

1 Cut the top piece from ¾-inch plywood to the length you've established. Here, the top and other components are all 12 inches deep. Nail the top to the ceiling.
2 Then cut the four verticals to fit between the floor and top. Attach adjustable shelf strips to the up-rights and nail the left and right uprights to the adjoining walls.
3 Install the remaining two verti-cals by toenailing them to the top piece and joining the bottoms to the back wall with angle irons.
4 Cut the 12-inch-deep shelves to the proper width, install clips on the shelf strips, and simply lay each shelf in place.
5 Use either wood putty or tape to finish all plywood edges.

Materials: To duplicate the unit here, you'll need 2½ sheets of ¾-inch plywood, eight 8-foot shelf strips, four 5-foot shelf strips, and clips.

3/4" PLYWOOD

3/4" PLYWOOD

ADJUSTABLE SHELF SUPPORTS

3/4" PLYWOOD

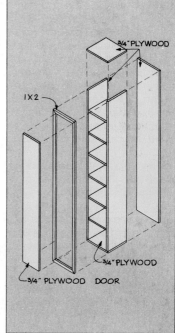

One of those "why-didn't-I-think-of-it" projects, this little box packs a big storage wallop. And it takes advantage of space that goes to waste in most every bathroom. Construction is simple, and you can use whatever material will look best in your bath. You can adjust the size, too, if the dimensions are too big for your bathroom situation.

1 Start by building a basic five-sided box with ¾-inch plywood. To duplicate this one exactly, cut the back 7½ inches wide and 46½ inches high. Cut the top and bottom 6x7½ inches and the sides 6x45 inches. Assemble with butt joints (see page 86) using white glue and finishing nails.

2 From ½-inch-thick plywood, cut the six shelves for the inside to 6x6 inches and nail in place. Or, if you prefer, cut them slightly narrower and install with adjustable shelf strips to support the shelves. Place the shelves so that you have 6 inches of clear space between each one.

3 Cut and apply 1x2 boards to the front edge of the storage unit. Miter the corners as shown here for the best appearance.

4 Measure the opening for the door and cut it to fit over the upper six compartments in the box. Use ¾-inch plywood and be sure to allow space for plywood edging tape as shown here.

5 Hang the door with pivot hinges (see page 93). They work well in a situation like this and present an unobtrusive appearance.

6 Install the toilet-paper holder in the compartment not covered by the door. Install pull and catch.

7 Hang the unit on the wall by simply screwing through the back into wall studs or anchors.

Materials: For project as shown, you'll need ½ sheet of ¾-inch plywood, ¼ sheet of ½-inch plywood, 6 feet of 1x2 facing, two pivot hinges, pull, catch, and toilet-paper holder.

CLUTTER CATCHING CORNER

If your bathroom is shy on storage space, these simple cabinets offer a lot. Plan them for any place you have free wall space. These are hung above a counter, but they could run floor to ceiling. Stock shutters eliminate the door-building job.

The two separate units are hung independently. Our instructions show you how to build the cabinet on the left.

1 Plan the overall dimensions according to the space you have and the size of the shutters you buy. Cut the surround from 1x6s and assemble the four sides with butt joints. Use white glue and finishing nails or wood screws.

2 Cut the vertical interior divider ¾ inch narrower than the frame to allow for shutters. Add shelf strips and cut shelves to fit.

3 Hinge two shutters together with the pivot on the inside. Then hang that pair and the third shutter on the inside of the 1x6 frame. Use butt hinges, mortised or unmortised (see page 93).

4 Apply a back of plywood or hardboard for extra strength. It can be inset or flush with equally good results.

5 All that's left is the hanging. Use long wood screws through the back into the studs or, without a back, hang the unit on ledger strips (see page 91).

Materials: To duplicate this one, you'll need 22 feet of 1x6s, three shutters (8x32 inches), eight shelf strips, six butt hinges, pulls, catches and one-fourth sheet of ¾-inch plywood for the back.

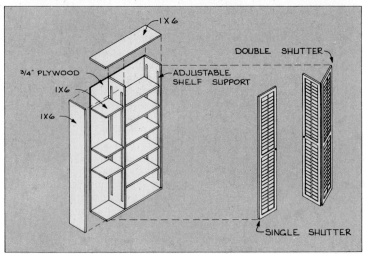

SEE-ALL STORAGE BANQUETTE

This high-style medicine cabinet will update any bathroom. See-into storage and a high-and-wide mirror help to visually maximize the space in cramped quarters. As you plan this project, be sure to concentrate on its installed height; you'll want to allow plenty of room to comfortably reach your lavatory faucets. The optional mirror adds to the total effect.

1 Plan the horizontal size so that the cabinet fits your lavatory-toilet wall. Cut pieces of the basic box from ¾-inch plywood; 12 inches square is a good size.

2 Plan verticals to divide the interior spaces and cut them to size. Rout grooves in the ends and in both sides of the dividers to receive the slide-up doors. Use a ⅜-inch router bit; make the grooves ¼-inch deep and ½-inch in from the top and front.

3 For the doors, cut a ⅛-inch slot in the edges of 1x2s. Then cut the 1x2s to make mitered door frames to the size you've worked out. Drill holes to receive ¼-inch dowels in the side pieces; drill 1-inch finger holes in bottom pieces. Assemble three sides, slip acrylic sheet in place, and attach the fourth side. Glue dowels in place so they protrude ¼ inch.

4 Assemble top, bottom, and one end of the basic box; add a door and a divider, positioning the dowels in the grooves. Repeat to the other end.

5 Hang the cabinet on ledger strips (page 91) cut to fit inside each compartment.

6 For mirror frame (optional), cut dado in 1x2s; then, cut 1x2s to fit around the mirror. Miter these joints to make your project look best. Glue and nail three sides of frame, insert mirror in dadoes, then attach fourth side. Mount on wall with clips or nails.

Materials: For a 4½-foot, 12-inch-high unit, you'll need one sheet of ¾-inch plywood, 16 feet of 1x2s, 5 square feet of acrylic sheet, and dowels.

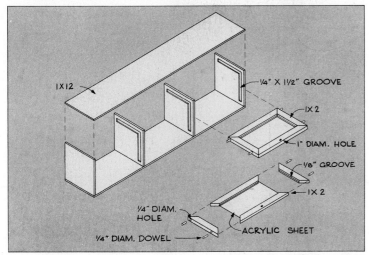

1X12
¼" X 1½" GROOVE
1X2
1" DIAM. HOLE
⅛" GROOVE
1X2
¼" DIAM. HOLE
¼" DIAM. DOWEL
ACRYLIC SHEET

LAUNDRY

Good storage in a good spot next to your laundry equipment earns its keep in more ways than one. Not only does it keep the necessities handy, it can speed your work and make it a lot more pleasant by helping keep everything neat. All the projects in this chapter will help corral the clutter; some also create a place to fold clean clothes and temporarily store dirty ones. The space you have for the washer and dryer may dictate which of the projects you can choose. But we have projects both large and small, so that one is sure to fit your situation. And, as with all of our projects, you can shrink or expand it to fit your needs, budget, and available space. Start by analyzing your laundry as it is now. Measure the space you have available, and be sure to note any complications caused by pipes. List your storage needs as definitely as possible, and pick the project that comes the closest to meeting those needs. Then round up your tools, gather the necessary materials, and you'll be on your way to a better, more convenient laundry that will make every trip there a lot easier.

HOLD & FOLD LAUNDRY CABINET

This simple laundry supply center can be assembled in short order. A commercial pre-finished sink base cabinet provides adequate storage space and clothes folding room, and a simple plywood surround unifies the whole area.

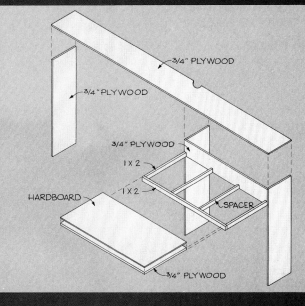

3/4" PLYWOOD

3/4" PLYWOOD

3/4" PLYWOOD

1 X 2

1 X 2

HARDBOARD

SPACER

3/4" PLYWOOD

1 Build the three-legged surround part of this unit from ¾-inch plywood. Cut the top piece wide enough to span the distance from the front of the control panel to the wall and cut notches for pipes and vent stack. Cut three legs to the same width and assemble with butt joints.

2 Attach 2x2 ledger to wall. Lift the surround into place and anchor to ledger with wood screws.

3 Place stock, pre-finished cabinet next to the laundry equipment, against the two right legs. Add a cut-to-fit piece of ¾-inch plywood to fill the gap between the cabinet and top board.

4 Make a framework of 1x2s to raise the counter top high enough to match the height of the washer top. Plan the framework to receive the ¾-inch plywood topper and a layer of ¼-inch hardboard. (The hardboard makes a good working surface and can be replaced easily.)

5 Attach framework and surfaces to the cabinet top from underneath with wood screws.

6 If your basement floor is uneven, or if the floor slopes because of the proximity to the drain, you may need to shim the cabinet slightly. Use scrap wood shingles and drive them under the cabinet edges until the surface is level. Then chisel off the exposed part of the shims.

Materials: With standard-size appliances, in addition to the stock base cabinet, you'll need one sheet of ¾-inch plywood, ¼ sheet of tempered hardboard, and 12 feet of 1x2s.

WASHDAY WORKHORSE

Lighten your laundry load with this clothes rack and storage shelf. The ceiling-suspended box keeps all supplies together and saves on floor space.

1 Choose the spot you want to use for this handy shelf/pole arrangement and measure between the outsides of ceiling joists.

2 Build the box from 1x10 boards. Cut top, bottom, and back to the length you've established. Assemble with butt joints. Then cut sides to fit in the same way.

3 Cut the two 1x4s to suspend the unit. You'll want to make them long enough to accommodate the person in your family with the shortest reach. Here, they're about three feet long. After cutting, round off the lower corners.

4 Cut the 1-inch-diameter clothes pole to length. It should be 1½ inches longer than the box. Drill two corresponding 1-inch-diameter holes in the ends of the 1x4s. This step is easiest if you line them up carefully and drill both at one time.

5 Nail the 1x4s to the outside of the box and apply glue to the clothes pole and slip it into place. Fasten the assembled unit to the ceiling joists with at least two wood screws on each side. you should space the 1x4s a minimum of 12 inches from the wall to allow adequate hanging space.

Materials: For a shelf/pole unit that spans three joists, you'll need 12 lineal feet of 1x10s, 6 feet of 1x4s, and a 3-foot length of clothes pole.

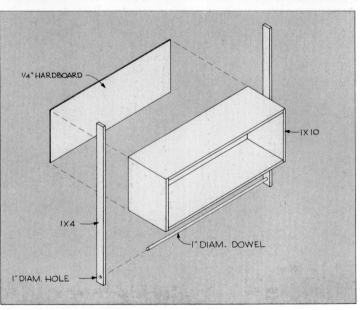

HAMPER-COUNTER, WITH SHELVES

This three-in-one unit is designed to blend in with the lines of your washer and dryer. An extra shelf mounted on the wall behind washer and dryer unifies the whole area.

1 Plan the dimensions of the unit by matching height, depth, and toe space with those of your washer and dryer. Draw those lines on a sheet of ¾-inch plywood and extend the 8-inch-deep back shelf support to a height 12 inches below the ceiling. Cut both sides to these dimensions.

2 Cut the floor, counter top, and top piece and assemble with butt joints. Also glue and nail the toe board in position.

3 Cut the fronts for the base and the upper section to fit, then mark the rounded openings and cut those with a saber saw.

4 Cut 1x1 ledger strips for the shelves and glue and nail in place. Then cut the three upper shelves (you can use the larger cutout) and slip into place.

5 Nail and glue the two front pieces into position.

6 Set the nails slightly below the surface; fill the holes and exposed plywood edges with wood putty and sand smooth.

7 (Optional) Cut a 1x8 to fit the top of your washer and dryer. Notch for pipes and vent stack. Install with metal shelf brackets.

Materials: For the project as shown, you'll need 2½ sheets of ¾-inch plywood, and 6 feet of 1x4s. (Optional shelf: 6 lineal feet of 1x8, and two shelf brackets.)

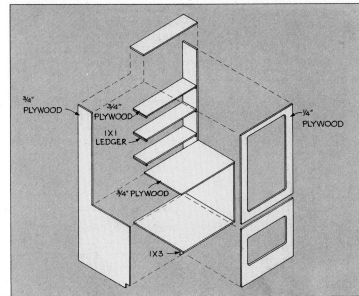

¾" PLYWOOD

¾" PLYWOOD

1X1 LEDGER

¼" PLYWOOD

¾" PLYWOOD

1X3

WASHDAY STORAGE, PLUS

This compact cabinet makes a super work spot for folding, mending, and storing laundry, while the spacious counter provides space for cutting out patterns and fabrics. Plus, you'll find the counter handy for dozens of other household projects. The closed storage below provides a home for all laundry supplies, and even your portable sewing machine.

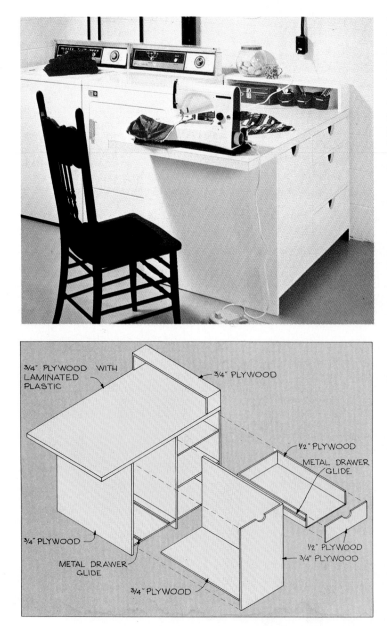

1 Plan the dimensions that will work best for you; the storage area could be as short.as the depth of your washer and dryer. But do plan the counter top overhang to be at least 12 inches in order to provide adequate knee space. Thirty-two inches makes a good height for a sewing table. Here, the cabinet part is 2 feet wide and 3 feet deep; the counter extends another foot.

2 Cut the sides, back, bottom, and the counter top from ¾-inch plywood. Assemble with glue and nails using butt joints. Then cut and install the interior vertical and horizontal dividers.

3 Apply the plastic laminate surface to the top and edges with contact cement. Trim and file the edges smooth.

4 Install drawer glides in basic cabinet following directions that are included in package (and see page 92).

5 Build the drawers like simple boxes from ½-inch plywood with butt joints (see page 85). Make hand hole cutouts with jigsaw. Measure carefully to make sure drawers will fit properly when installed with drawer glides.

6 Cut rear ledge from 1x6s. Using butt joints, glue, and nails, assemble and attach to counter top. Or it can simply be set in place.

7 Fill nail holes and edges of plywood with wood putty.

Materials: For the fabric center you'll need two sheets of ¾-inch plywood, one half-sheet of ½-inch plywood, 3 feet of 1x6s, plastic laminate and adhesive, and drawer glides.

WRAPAROUND LAUNDRY CENTER

This simple laundry center provides essential storage space in a minimal 7x6 foot area. The outside units are topless and backless and have one permanent base shelf, while the others adjust. The center section is a skinny backless box with door.

1 Position laundry equipment to allow room for the narrow center cabinet and clearance for plumbing and vent pipes.

2 Attach 2x2 furring strips to wall. Cut perforated hardboard to size; glue and nail to furring strips. (You may have to use thicker furring to clear water pipes or electrical conduit.)

3 Cut verticals from ¾-inch plywood. Notch to receive header. Install shelf standards on insides of tall verticals.

4 Cut 1x8 header to span entire unit. Glue and nail header to verticals. Cut shelves from 1x12s. Attach one 4 inches from floor at the bottom of both tall modules by nailing from outside. Lift unit into position. Install shelf clips and adjustable shelves.

5 Cut pieces for center cabinet from ¾-inch plywood and 1x8. Using butt joints, glue and nail verticals to horizontals. Then, attach door with two loose pin hinges and install magnetic catch and door pull. Place in position.

Materials: You'll need 2½ sheets of ¾-inch plywood, 10 feet of 1x8s, 16 feet of 1x12s, 16 feet of 2x2s, one sheet of perforated hardboard, shelf standards and clips, two hinges, catch, and pull.

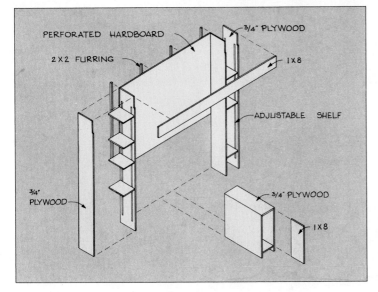

PERFORATED HARDBOARD

¾" PLYWOOD

2 X 2 FURRING

1 X 8

ADJUSTABLE SHELF

¾" PLYWOOD

¾" PLYWOOD

1 X 8

KIDS' BEDROOMS

Easing the storage squeeze in a child's bedroom can be more than just solving a problem—it can be fun, too. All the projects in this chapter do their job well—whether they make a spot for toys, store the clothes the closet won't hold, or just organize all the possessions so many kids accumulate.

And some designs are especially adaptable to the changing needs every youngster experiences as only a year or two rolls by.

The fun comes in the finishing and placement of the projects you build. Painting these units in bright colors will add spark to almost any room. Or choose white to give the area a lighter, more contemporary look.

The spot you choose for the project can make a walloping difference in the room, too. One of the wall-hung units in this chapter can add depth and interest to a plain wall. Others can be placed in the center of a room to divide the space and virtually create a new environment for your child.

So, solve the storage problem—and make your kids' rooms in your house better places to be.

TRIPLE UNIT
STACKING
SYSTEM

Three modified boxes can turn a child's room into a parents dream. These store-alls can be stacked for a toddler, as shown then rearranged as a counter later on, or even dispersed to all parts of the room.

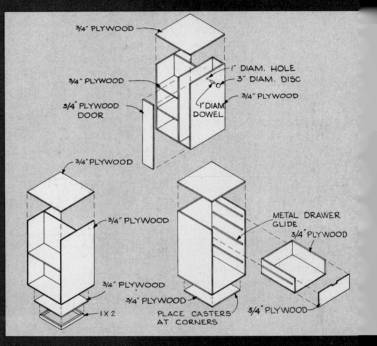

3/4" PLYWOOD

3/4" PLYWOOD

1" DIAM. HOLE
3" DIAM. DISC
3/4" PLYWOOD

3/4" PLYWOOD
DOOR

1" DIAM.
DOWEL

3/4" PLYWOOD

3/4" PLYWOOD

METAL DRAWER
GLIDE
3/4" PLYWOOD

3/4" PLYWOOD

3/4" PLYWOOD
1 X 2

PLACE CASTERS
AT CORNERS

3/4" PLYWOOD

1 For each of the three units, build a four-sided box to get started. These are 24 inches square and 36 inches high. Use either ¾-inch particleboard or plywood, and assemble with butt joints.

2 For the lower left unit, add a vertical divider in the center and one shelf on each side.

3 To duplicate the upper unit, install the full vertical divider 6 inches away from one side and add a recessed back to that compartment. Then cut and install the other vertical divider and add two shelves on each side. Cut the tall door and install hinges and a touch latch. Drill a hole for the ¾-inch dowel and the round re-

tainer, and glue in place.
4 For the lower right cube, build a 12-inch-deep drawer, divide the remaining space into three equal parts, and build drawers for that space. Use simple box construction (page 92), cut the hand holes with a jig saw, and install with drawer glides (page 92).
5 Take your choice of bases. Cut ¾-inch material to a 22-inch square and add plate casters, or make a recessed frame of 1x2s.

Materials: To duplicate the project shown here, you'll need five sheets of ¾-inch plywood or particleboard, 8 feet of 1x2s, drawer glides, plate casters, hinges, latch, and a scrap of dowel.

STORAGE FOR THE SHORT AND TALL

Shelves like these help any youngster keep organized. Low level storage provides a place for the smallest child to stash books and toys. And as he gets taller, all shelves will become easily accessible.

1 Build the basic shell of the tall unit first. Here, it's 5 feet high, 3 feet wide, and 9 inches deep, but you can easily adjust dimensions if necessary. Use ¾-inch plywood and install a flush or inset back of ¼-inch plywood.

2 Cut the two lower shelves to fit and saw dadoes for the 9-inch-high, ½-inch plywood dividers. Install this unit.

3 For the upper part, install the full width shelf with 3-inch-wide skirts for extra strength. Cut and attach the 3-foot vertical divider.

4 Screw the adjustable shelf strips in place, and cut and add the shelves and the single door.

5 Build the 7-inch-deep base. Here the wood is 2x2, but you might use 1x4s on edge if you want to clear the baseboard behind the unit.

6 Set the unit on the base and drive screws through the back into the wall studs.

7 Build the side unit like a five-sided box. Plan it 9 inches high, 9 inches deep, and as long as you like. Install the ¾-inch dividers and attach unit to the wall.

Materials: To duplicate this project, you'll need 1½ sheets of ¾-inch plywood, one-half sheet of ½-inch plywood, one sheet of ¼-inch plywood, 5 feet of 2x2s, shelf strips, and hinges.

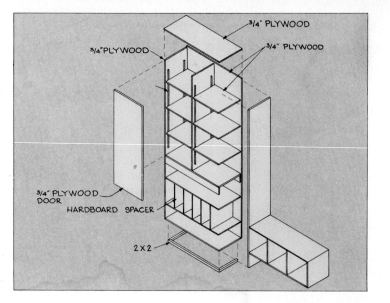

AN OPEN OR CLOSED CASE

This compact play environment is a natural for active kids. It closes to keep the clutter of toys and games neatly hidden—and casters on both sides make it easy to move where the action is from room to room.

The two sides are built separately and hinged together. Adjustable shelves on both sides give the play center added flexibility.

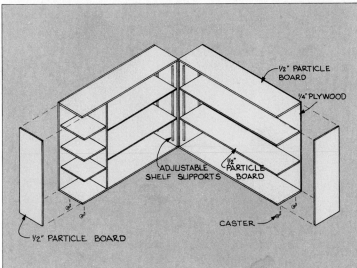

½" PARTICLE BOARD

¼" PLYWOOD

½" PARTICLE BOARD

ADJUSTABLE SHELF SUPPORTS

½" PARTICLE BOARD

CASTER

1 Begin by building two large boxes that make up the exterior of the unit. Here, they are 4 feet wide, 3 feet high, and 1 foot deep. You can alter the sizes, but plan a depth of at least a foot. Cut the sides, tops, and bottoms from particleboard, and the backs from ¼-inch plywood.

2 Assemble both boxes with butt joints and attach the flush backs with white glue and finishing nails.

3 For the interior of the right unit, simply install shelf strips (page 91) and cut the shelves to length.

4 For the left unit, cut and install the vertical divider; then cut and install the three fixed 12x12-inch shelves. In the other section, add shelf strips and cut shelves to fit as you did in the previous step.

5 Attach casters to all four corners of each unit. Buy the platform type in any size you want—generally, the larger the better—and select them for the type of floor covering they'll be rolling on. Also, you may want to put one locking caster on each unit.

6 Place the two units together and install 2-inch butt hinges on one end to join them.

7 On the other end, screw a hasp to the joint to keep the unit closed when the kids (or you) are too busy to tidy up the shelves.

Materials: To build the closable unit shown, you'll need two sheets of ½-inch particleboard, one sheet of ¼-inch plywood, eight platform casters (four of the locking type), one pair of butt hinges, shelf strips, and a hasp.

BOX STORAGE PLUS BUNK BEDS

These wall-hung boxes make a modular storage/study center that fits just about anywhere. You can build several and arrange them to fill most any space. Then, as a finishing touch, build and install the bunk beds. You can even fit the whole system into a small room—just experiment with the arrangement until it makes the most of the wall space you have.

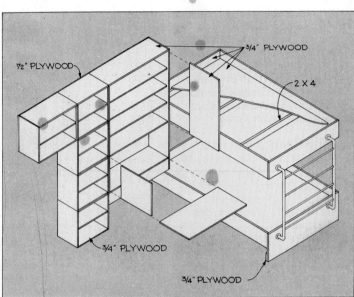

1 Build the smaller boxes 18 inches square and 12 inches deep. For simplest construction, use butt joints with flush backs. For the open boxes, make shelves the same depth as the sides.

2 Cut the sides, top, and bottom of the larger unit. It measures 3x5 feet and is also 12 inches deep. Assemble with the bottom inset 6 inches, and cut and add a 6-inch skirt below the bottom. Add the back, install the upper shelves and doors, and attach the unit to the wall. Cut the 18-inch-deep desk top and attach piano hinge and drop-leaf support hardware.

3 Build the upper bunk with 9-inch plywood sides. The inside of the twin-size bunk should measure 39x72 inches. Add a plywood bottom, four 2x4 crosspieces as shown, and then another sheet of plywood on top.

4 For the lower bunk, follow the same procedure, but substitute 14-inch-high ends and omit the bottom piece of plywood. Add a 4-inch-wide piece of plywood at the bottom of each end.

5 Set the lower bunk in position and then with help, position upper bunk approximately 4½ feet high. Drive lag screws through into wall studs, then attach the heavy-duty grab bar assembly to support the foot—and serve as the access ladder.

Materials: For the project as shown, you'll need seven sheets of ¾-inch plywood, 1½ sheets of ½-inch plywood, a piano hinge, pivot hinges, drop-leaf hardware, pulls, catches and the special-order heavy-duty grab bar.

A KID-TAILORED CLOSET

This simple arrangement converts any wide closet into a well-organized wardrobe space. Build it from scratch with our instructions, or substitute a ready-made chest of drawers. Either way, the closet will hold lots more than it did with its old one-pole, one-shelf setup.

1 Build the boxlike surround to divide the space. This one is 2 feet square and nearly touches the ceiling inside. Use ¾-inch plywood or particle board and assemble the back, sides, and bottom with butt joints.

2 Cut the upper shelves and the drawer dividers. The drawer dividers will work best spaced about 8 inches apart.

3 Construct the six drawers according to the dimensions you've established. Choose the construction method and glide arrangement that will work best for you (see page 92).

4 Remove the back baseboard in the closet, if necessary, and slip the center unit in place. It's not necessary to fasten it to the wall.

5 Establish the best heights for the three clothes poles. Hang them by drilling into the sides of the center unit and using holders on the outer walls.

6 Cut the lower right shelf to fit and install with ledger strips.

Materials: For the unit shown, you'll need four sheets of ¾-inch plywood, one sheet of ½-inch plywood, 6 feet of 1-inch clothes pole, 3 clothes-pole holders, and hardware for six drawers.

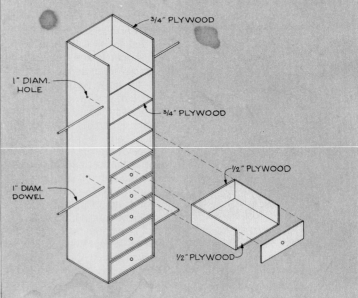

3/4" PLYWOOD

1" DIAM. HOLE

3/4" PLYWOOD

1" DIAM. DOWEL

1/2" PLYWOOD

1/2" PLYWOOD

DOUBLE-DUTY DOUBLE DECKER

Here's a high-level bunk bed arrangement that brings plenty of storage along with it. Use it to take advantage of unused space in the middle of a room.

1 Build the wall unit first. Plan it 12 inches deep, as high as your ceiling, and wide enough on the inside to receive the mattress you'll use (a twin size is 39 inches). Use ¾-inch plywood. Assemble the framework and then add the dividers.

2 Next, build the chest. Make four drawer support frames from 2x2s as shown in the drawing. (Here, the chest is 18 inches deep.)

3 Assemble the sides, back, and front frame with the drawer supports. Build the four drawers and add center glides (see page 92).

4 Build a frame of 2x4s the same size as your mattress. With help, put chest and frame in position. Attach frame to the inside of the wall unit with lag screws and screw it to the chest. Then cover the frame with a 6-foot-long sheet of ¾-inch plywood. For the sides and foot, nail on 12-inch-wide pieces of plywood.

5 For the ladder, assemble a 2x4 frame 14 inches wide with a 1-inch dowel placed every 12 inches. For a fireman's pole, you can use any 3-inch-diameter metal pipe. Cut it to size and attach with flanges.

Materials: To build the units shown, you'll need four sheets of ¾-inch plywood, 2 sheets of ½-inch plywood, 30 feet of 2x4s, 48 feet of 2x2s, 10 feet of 1-inch dowels, and 8 feet of 3-inch pipe.

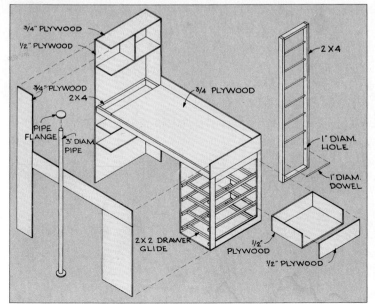

STORAGE FOR STUDY—WITH A DESK, TOO

These desk and upper level storage units adapt to any wall. Plan the sizes to fit a corner of your child's room and turn it into a convenient study nook. Open-front storage without drawers makes the project a snap to build.

These units are all made of plywood. A top sheet of acrylic gives the desk a smooth work surface.

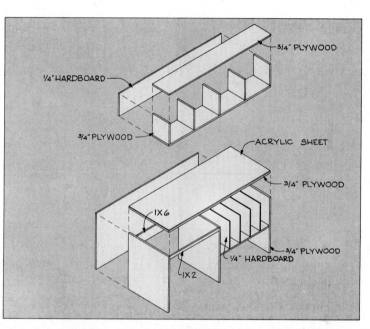

1 Work out the size you need first, but plan the desk 30 inches high and 24 inches deep. This one is 5 feet long; you can adjust this dimension either way, but keep the desk's kneehole at least 28 inches wide for comfort.

2 Cut the desk top, back, and the three verticals from ¾-inch plywood and assemble with butt joints. Use white glue and screws or finishing nails.

3 Cut and install a 6-inch-wide piece of plywood at the top near the back of the knee space for extra strength, and nail in a 1x2 across the front for appearance.

4 Then cut the right side horizontal shelf and dividers; these dividers are 14 inches high. Nail and glue the horizontal in place first, then add the dividers.

5 Build the wall-hung unit 10 inches high and 10 inches deep. Use butt joints for the simplest construction. Assemble like a five-sided box and add dividers to the interior.

6 Hang the upper unit at a convenient, reachable height. Drive long wood screws through the back into the wall studs, or use one of the other hanging methods shown on page 90.

7 As the last step, install the acrylic sheet work surface. You can buy one cut to the exact size and have the edges polished.

Materials: For the size shown, you'll need 2½ sheets of ¾-inch plywood, one sheet of ¼-inch hardboard, and a 2x5-foot acrylic sheet.

PARENTS' BEDROOMS

Good storage in anyone's master bedroom can mean a real turnaround in total convenience. It takes only a little effort to make full use of existing storage space, and just a bit more effort to create storage where you never thought it was possible. With the projects in this chapter you'll get more than just a place for everything; you'll get the organization, access, and visibility you need.

Some of the projects can change a room completely. By using a new storage unit as a divider, you can make the room function in a great new way. Or a closet can become a dressing center as well as just storage for clothes.

So consider the total effect you want to create and then start adapting these projects to fit your own situation. Some are simple enough to build and install in a single weekend. Others will take a little longer, even though they're not at all difficult. Whatever projects you choose, the time and effort you invest will pay off in convenience every day for a long time to come. You'll wonder why you put up with the storage hassle in your bedroom for as long as you did!

A STACK OF SPECTACULAR SHELVES

This is one way to cash in on a closet. The shelf space that this project adds to a bedroom can store so much more than a large chest—and help you free up floor space in the bargain.

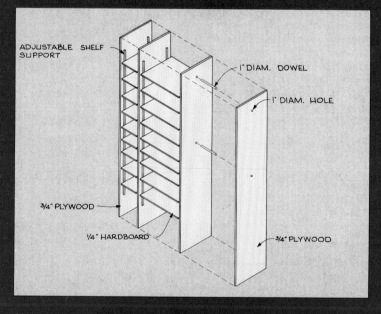

ADJUSTABLE SHELF SUPPORT

1" DIAM. DOWEL

1" DIAM. HOLE

3/4" PLYWOOD

1/4" HARDBOARD

3/4" PLYWOOD

1 Plan the sizes of the shelves and uprights according to the interior dimensions of the existing closet. Here, the closet is 24 inches deep and the unit only 18. This closet also has its own ceiling; if yours doesn't, you may want to add a continuous shelf across the top for extra storage space. And, of course, adjust the spacing of the two middle verticals to the width of your space.

2 Cut the four vertical pieces to the best size for your closet. If your closet has a baseboard, be sure to notch out the back to allow for it. Add the adjustable shelf strips and drill clothes pole holes before installing. Then nail the end panels to the inside of the closet walls. To install the two middle panels, screw small angle irons to the panel and the wall, and toenail the

panels to the ceiling or continuous shelf.

3 Cut the 1/4-inch hardboard shelves. Here, those on the left are 9 inches wide, and the others are 22 inches wide. (Decorative note: you may want to consider covering the shelves with colorful self-adhesive vinyl, as was done here. You'll get a very washable surface and sidestep a lengthy painting job.)

4 Cut the two clothes poles to length, apply glue, and slip the poles into place.

Materials: To duplicate this unit, you'll need two sheets of 3/4-inch plywood, 1½ sheets of 1/4-inch hardboard, 3 feet of clothes pole, shelf strips and clips, angle irons, screws, and nails.

EXTRA SPACE IN THE SAME OLD CLOSET

Here's a build-and-install storage idea that really stacks up. This four-door unit capitalizes on the vertical space that women's clothes so often waste. And it offers an opportunity to rearrange the closet poles so no hanging space is sacrificed.

1 Build the center part with ¾-inch plywood. Here, the sides are 18 inches deep and 8 feet tall. The shelves are 14 inches wide and spaced 18 inches apart. Cut the shelves ¾ inch shorter than the sides to allow for the doors.

2 Cut the four doors to fit and install with your choices of hinges and touch latches (see page 93). For the fronts, choose acrylic sheet mirrors (you can have them cut at your dealer) and simply glue them to the plywood doors.

3 Remove the old pole and shelf and slide the unit in place, centering it in the closet. Add two shelves on each side by installing them with cleats on each end.

4 Cut clothes poles to fit and install at least 12 inches from the back closet wall.

5 Cut the shoe shelf 3 inches longer than the depth of the cabinet to allow for the slope, and attach to wall and center section with cleats. Attach the quarter round toward back of shelf for heel rest.

Materials: For the project as shown, you'll need two sheets of ¾-inch plywood, 3 lineal feet of 1x4s, 2 feet of quarter round, clothes poles, acrylic mirrors, wood glue, and finishing nails.

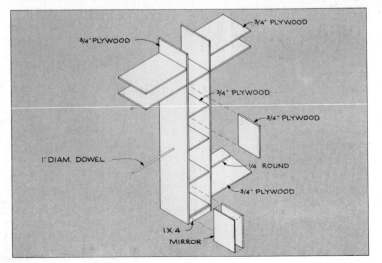

3/4" PLYWOOD
3/4" PLYWOOD
3/4" PLYWOOD
3/4" PLYWOOD
1" DIAM. DOWEL
1/4 ROUND
3/4" PLYWOOD
1X4
MIRROR

SUPER STORAGE TO SLEEP OVER

How many times have you stuffed things under an ordinary bed and then wished you could take advantage of that space in an organized way. This project does exactly that— with king-sized drawers. Our drawing shows a stud wall used as both a headboard and a room divider. Add it if you like, or build the bed to fit against an existing wall.

1 Plan the size according to your mattress and cut the platform one inch larger on all four sides. For a double mattress, make it 56x77 inches. Use an oversize piece of plywood normally sold for Ping-Pong tabletops, or use two pieces of ¾-inch fir plywood.

2 Build the base to allow for a 3-inch toe space on the sides and foot of the bed from 2x4s on edge.

3 Cut three 8-inch uprights the same dimension as the width of your platform and two head-to-foot 30-inch-long dividers to fit between them. This framework forms the division for the drawers and supports the platform. Space it so the platform overhangs equally at head and foot.

4 Assemble base, framework, and platform with glue and finishing nails. If you've planned a 2-piece platform, the joint must fall over the center upright.

5 Build the four drawers to fit the openings and install with heavy-duty metal glides (see page 92).

6 To attach the 10-inch-high foot, first cut a spacer board to the same length as the width of your platform and as wide as the overhang. Nail it to the top of the base, then glue and nail the foot to it and the platform edge.

7 Cut and attach the oversize false drawer fronts with white glue and screws driven from the inside.

Materials: For a double bed, you'll need four sheets of ¾-inch plywood, one sheet of ½-inch plywood, 20 lineal feet of 2x4s, and four pairs of drawer glides.

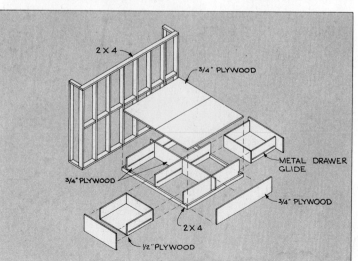

2 X 4

¾" PLYWOOD

¾" PLYWOOD

METAL DRAWER GLIDE

¾" PLYWOOD

2 X 4

½" PLYWOOD

ALL AROUND THE BED STORAGE

Call it a headboard, a mini-library, or whatever you like. This storage unit gives you a spot to keep lots of things close at hand and its built-in look will add flair to any bedroom.

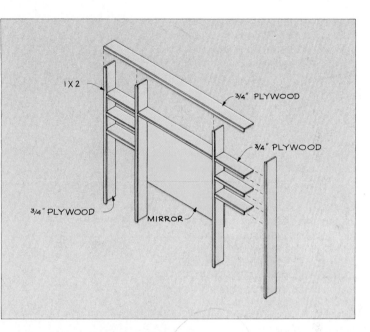

1 Cut the four verticals to your floor-to-ceiling measurement, less the thickness of the top piece. Use either 1x8s or ¾-inch plywood for this project. Notch the bottoms for baseboards, if needed.

2 Assemble the two side units of the project. Cut shelves to fit the space you have (or the width of your bedside tables), and install with cleats.

3 Slip the units in place (if your bedroom has a ceiling molding, remove it first), and then cut the top piece and tap it into position. Toenail the uprights to it and drive four finishing nails into the ceiling for stability.

4 Next install the long center shelf. Cut it to fit and attach it with cleats on each end.

5 Have a mirror cut to size (it will be your biggest expense for this project), and install with mirror clips anchored in the wall. Or you can have the glass dealer drill holes for installation with rosettes if you like.

6 Apply the 1x2 trim to the fronts of the shelves and uprights. Do the uprights first, using white glue and finishing nails. Then cut the trim for the shelves and finish this step.

7 Nail a trim piece to the ceiling board. Use a 1x2, or add a curved molding to duplicate that of the rest of the room.

Materials: For a 9-foot-wide unit, you'll need 52 lineal feet of 1x8s, 52 lineal feet of 1x2s, and the mirror (consider a less expensive grade for this project).

HEADBOARD FULL OF DRAWERS

There's a heap of storage in this giant headboard. It takes careful workmanship, but the drawer space you'll gain is well worth the effort.

1 The basic construction is just a large box. Here it's 7 feet long, 4 feet high, and 16 inches deep, but you can alter the size to fit your bed's width and the room size. Cut the drawer side of the box to the size you want, then divide up the spaces for the drawers. Saw those cutouts with a saber saw.

2 Assemble the top, bed side, bottom, and drawer side with butt joints. Then add vertical dividers to interior. Our drawing shows bookshelves on each end; you can alter that just by changing the location of the end dividers.

3 Build and install the drawers as shown on page 92. For the look this unit has, use overlapping false fronts for the drawers.

4 The base is a simple mitered frame of 2x4s. Make yours so that it's recessed 2 inches on all sides.

5 Build the decorative top piece like a five-sided shallow box, slightly shallower than the depth of the overall unit. For the best appearance, use miter joints. Attach with screws from below.

6 Install the bookshelves in the end compartments (see page 91).

Materials: To build the project as shown, you'll need six sheets of ¾-inch plywood (here, the two for front and back are hardwood faced), three sheets of ½-inch plywood, two sheets of ¼-inch plywood, 18 lineal feet of 2x4s, and 12 pairs of drawer glides.

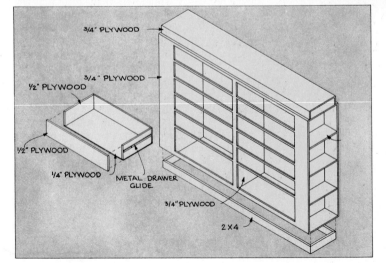

3/4" PLYWOOD
3/4" PLYWOOD
1/2" PLYWOOD
1/2" PLYWOOD
1/4" PLYWOOD
METAL DRAWER GLIDE
3/4" PLYWOOD
2 X 4

A MAN'S MULTIPLE CLOSET

Most closets waste a lot of space when they're devoted to men's clothing. This project does away with waste and adds a bonus mini-dresser in the bargain.

1 Remove the existing clothes pole and shelf, measure the interior space you have, and plan the size of the dresser unit. It should be at least 15 inches wide, as this one is, and up to 24 inches deep. Plan the height for 7 feet.

2 Cut the L-shaped sides from a sheet of ¾-inch plywood with the dresser surface 4 feet from the floor and 15 inches deep.

3 Cut the horizontal shelves and assemble unit with butt joints.

4 Build and install the two drawers. Use ½-inch plywood with simple butt joints and mount with drawer glides.

5 Now just slip the unit in place, with equal spaces on each side. If your closet has a baseboard, notch out the back to allow for it. There's no need to fasten the unit to the wall.

6 Have a mirror cut to size and attach it to the wall with clips.

7 Now cut and install the four short clothes poles. Position the lower poles high enough for jackets and shirts to clear the floor, then repeat for the upper two. This way, the higher reach will be minimized.

Materials: For the project as shown, you'll need one sheet of ¾-inch plywood, 1½ sheets of ½-inch plywood, two pairs of drawer glides, 10 feet of clothes pole, and a mirror.

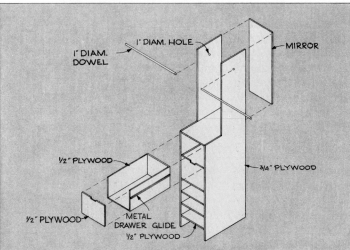

1" DIAM. HOLE

1" DIAM. DOWEL

MIRROR

½" PLYWOOD

¾" PLYWOOD

½" PLYWOOD

METAL DRAWER GLIDE

½" PLYWOOD

LIVING
DINING
FAMILY
ROOMS

These rooms all lend themselves to storage projects that can perform several jobs at once. Each design provides new space for the things you need close to the areas where you need them. But beyond that, they spark new interest in dull or ordinary rooms. Some shelf arrangements can become the focal point of your room; other projects help divide large spaces so a room will function better.

Start by considering the objects that give you the biggest problems, whether there's no good place for them or the spot you have is inconvenient. Then examine the spaces the room has to offer. If your big problem is books, for instance, look to either the living room or family room and decide if wall space is your best bet, if a divider would make use of wasted floor space, or if the area behind a freestanding sofa offers the most potential for added storage.

The extra storage projects in this chapter will help you make your living, family, or dining room more complete. You can adjust the size of any of them to fit your situation—or build them in pairs.

SHOW-OFF HARDWOOD SHELVES

These hardwood shelves not only give you needed storage; they're also an attractive display for books, sculpture, and other objects. The two-inch-thick material and exposed screws enhance the structure.

Though hardwoods are the most durable and free from knots, you may choose cheaper lumber—such as rough or smooth fir—to achieve a more rustic look.

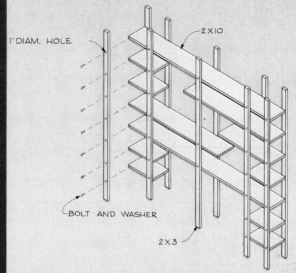

1" DIAM. HOLE

2X10

BOLT AND WASHER

2X3

1 Plan your unit by sketching a shelf-and-post arrangement to scale on paper. This one is 7 feet high and 7 feet wide, with seven equally spaced shelves on each end. Plan for any special things you'll want on the shelves, and then transfer the plan to the wall by sticking masking tape where each shelf will be.

2 Cut and sand all of the 2x3 support posts. They should be cut 1 inch lower than the ceiling. Cut and sand all of the 2x10 shelves you've planned.

3 Drill large holes for the recessed washers and screw heads. The diameter should be the same as the washers you'll use, and the depth equal to the thickness of the washer and head of the lag screw.

4 Lay shelves on edge across the floor in proper relation to your shelf plan. Position the front posts on the shelves.

5 Drill ⅜-inch pilot holes through the center of the posts' wide edges on into the shelves to a depth of 2½ to 3 inches.

6 Insert washers and drive hex-head, 3-inch lag screws through the posts into the shelves.

7 Turn the unit over (you'll need some help to keep it square). Position the back posts and attach them with nails and glue. Drill pilot holes before you drive the nails for best results.

Materials: For a project this size you'll need 80 lineal feet of 2x3s, 36 lineal feet of 2x10s, and 32 hex-head lag screws and washers.

A DIVIDER THAT EARNS ITS KEEP

Put this easy, inexpensive divider wherever you need help to define a certain area. It'll do that job nicely, and provide wide-open storage space at the same time.

1 Build a framework of 2x2s in the shape of a giant inverted U. The size shown—6½ feet high, 4 feet wide, and 10 inches deep is very usable.

2 Cover the top and ends with ⅛-inch hardboard and then apply the U-shaped front and back. For appearance's sake, duplicate the 18-inch depth shown in the top section. Also cover the insides of each end with hardboard.

3 Build two 10-inch-high, four-sided boxes from 1x12 lumber. Make these to a length that will fit snugly between the two ends. Use miter joints for the best appearance, (see page 87), but the simpler butt joints will also work.

4 Install these two boxes by nailing through the ends into the 2x2 framework. You can plan the projection on one side only as shown in the drawing, or split it equally between front and back. Allow 10 inches above the top box and the same space between them.

5 Next build two 10x15-inch boxes out of 1x12 material. Leave the ends out of one, enclose the other with a back and a side- or top-hinged door, and simply set them in place.

Materials: To build the project shown, you'll need two sheets of ⅛-inch hardboard, 30 lineal feet of 1x12, 36 lineal feet 2x2s, and one pair of hinges.

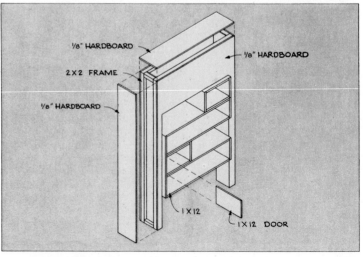

⅛" HARDBOARD
⅛" HARDBOARD
2 X 2 FRAME
⅛" HARDBOARD
1 X 12
1 X 12 DOOR

Build this hutch for your dining room—or place it as a room divider to create a dining area where you don't have one. You can use a dressy, hardwood-faced plywood for a fine furniture appearance, like this one, or choose a more inexpensive plywood for a painted finish. Either way, the simple lines look great in any setting.

1 Construct the 18-inch-deep outside shell first. Here, the width is 6½ feet and the height is 7 feet. Install a two-piece back (see how to make all joints on page 85) and fasten the full-width horizontal shelf in place at table height (usually 30 inches).

2 Tackle the rest of the project on a divide-and-conquer basis. Install the vertical dividers in the lower part, and then the cross pieces below the drawers. Cut and install the lower doors and shelves (see page 93).

3 Build the three 6-inch-deep drawers and install with metal glides (see page 92).

4 Divide the upper part with the two equally spaced 12-inch-deep verticals.

5 Make the upper shelves adjustable by using the unobtrusive dowel support method (see page 90). Or, use strips and clips for an easier installation.

Materials: For a project of the dimensions shown, you'll need five sheets of ¾-inch plywood (either AA fir or hardwood veneered), one sheet of ½-inch plywood, three pairs of drawer glides, six pairs of hinges, and nine pulls.

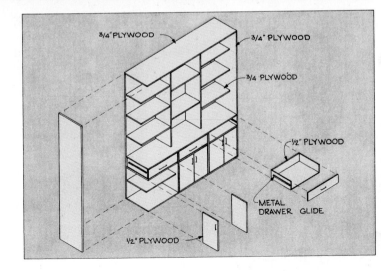

3/4" PLYWOOD

3/4" PLYWOOD

3/4 PLYWOOD

½" PLYWOOD

METAL DRAWER GLIDE

½" PLYWOOD

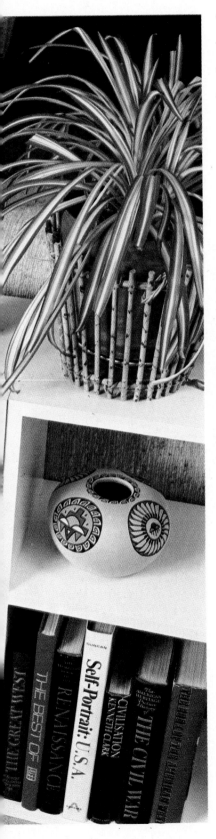

SPACE-SAVER STORAGE CUBES

Using a sofa as a room divider not only breaks down long rooms into usable living spaces, but provides a great spot for these handy, open-sided storage cubes, too.

Whether you stack them or set them on any of their sides, clean design gives them the versatility to go anywhere. Build them in multiples—two or three are as easy as one.

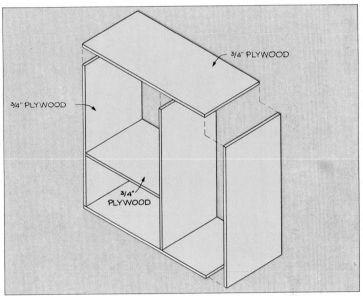

3/4" PLYWOOD

3/4" PLYWOOD

3/4" PLYWOOD

1 Plan your cubes to fit neatly behind your sofa by adjusting the size to the sofa back. Here, the cubes are 24 inches square and 11 inches deep—a size that adapts well to other locations, too. If you adjust sizes, make sure they remain square; this way, the cubes can be easily rearranged.

2 Cut the four sides 24x11 inches with 45-degree angles on the ends for miter joints (see page 87). Since these cubes are built without backs, miter joints and dado shelf construction (below) give the cubes extra strength. But, use butt joints (see page 85) if you prefer, or if you'll use the cubes for light storage only.

3 Determine the placement of the inside divider shelves and cut dadoes in the sides to receive the shelves. (One shelf will require a dado also.)

4 Assemble the sides, using white glue and finishing nails. Corner clamps will speed your work and help you get good accurate joints. Countersink the nails.

5 Measure, cut, and assemble the two shelves. Apply white glue to the dadoes, slip the vertical member in place, and nail it. Then fit the shorter horizontal shelf in place and nail.

6 Fill the nail holes, apply wood veneer tape to the edges or fill them with water putty, and sand lightly.

Materials: For each storage cube as shown, you'll need ½ sheet of plywood (4x4 feet) and edging tape or water putty.

CEILING-HIGH BOOKCASES

These simple, stately bookcases can turn a nothing wall into something really great. Use one or more of them on any wall where awkwardly placed windows make furniture arrangement difficult, and plan the widths to fit the space. Or build a series of them for a blank wall. The shelves shouldn't be wider than 48 inches if you plan to load them with books.

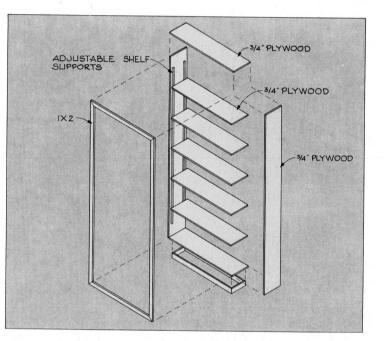

ADJUSTABLE SHELF SUPPORTS

3/4" PLYWOOD

3/4" PLYWOOD

3/4" PLYWOOD

1X2

1 Plan the vertical dimensions first. Make the recessed base as high as your baseboards. In most cases, a 3½-inch height will clear baseboards, but if your home has old-fashioned high bases, you'll need to notch the back of the cabinet. This cut will be ¾-inch deep and as high as your baseboard, less 3½ inches for the cabinet base. The bookcase itself should be 1 inch shorter than your base-to-ceiling measurement.

Build the base from ¾-inch plywood with butt or miter joints. Allow a 2-inch recess on the front and both ends, and ¾ inch in the rear.

If you plan to paint this structure, use pine facing and ledger strips, and birch plywood for the other parts. Lumber-core plywood would be your best choice since it has higher tensile strength for shelving.

2 Cut the 9-inch-deep vertical sides. Now's the time to plan the shelf support system. If you choose dadoes (see page 86), cut them into the sides at this point. Or use adjustable shelf support strips. In this case, you can inset them into the inside surface of the verticals for the best appearance. Or you can simply screw the strips to the verticals.

3 Cut the top and bottom; sand and assemble the frame with butt joints. Fit the top between the two sides and use white glue and finishing nails or screws.

4 Cut the 8¾-inch-deep shelves to length, and if you've chosen dadoed joints, glue and nail the shelves in place at this point. With adjustable shelf strips, it is wise to cut the shelves 3/16 inch shorter than the inside clearance for easy removal.

5 Cut 1x2 facing to fit around the outer frame. Use miter joints for these trim pieces to make your project look best. Attach the trim with finishing nails.

6 Fasten the base to the bottom shelf of the bookcase. (Remember to leave your 2-inch backset on front and two sides.) Now carefully slide the entire unit (less shelves, if adjustable) into place. That extra inch at the ceiling makes it easy.

7 To install, just position and check for level. If necessary shim with wedges until level then toenail into floor with finishing nails.

8 Secure the upper part to the wall by attaching a 1x1¼-inch cleat to the wall and to the underside of the top shelf. Mount the cleat on the wall first using finishing nails (see page 91), then drive three 4d finishing nails down through the top shelf into the strip.

9 Build narrow bookcase shown at left of photo in same manner.

10 If using shelf support strips, insert clips in slots and position shelves.

Materials: For the 32-inch-wide bookcase shown, you'll need one 4x8-foot sheet of ¾-inch plywood (preferably lumber-core birch), 28 feet of 1x2s, and shelf supports and clips (optional).

SLIP-TOGETHER SHELVES

Take out a few screws, flip open some latches, and this entire unit slips apart for easy moving or storage. And, it's just as easy to build, being mostly a matter of cutting a few notches, attaching suitcase latches, then just slipping it all together.

1 Start by cutting six 1x8s 78 inches long for uprights.

2 Cut five 1x12 shelves 60 inches long and one 34 inches. (NOTE: Any wood is acceptable. If you plan to paint these shelves, pine lumber is a good choice.)

3 Cut a pair of 3-inch-deep, 13/16-inch-wide notches 4 inches from either end and in the center of one long shelf. Use this as a pattern to cut notches in the remaining shelves.

4 On one edge of the uprights, cut the same size notches starting 6 inches from the bottom and every 12 inches thereafter.

5 Cut 1x2s to 4 feet. Cut 45-degree angles going opposite ways at either end of the 1x2s.

6 On the floor, assemble as shown in the drawing.

7 Install the nine suitcase latches on the uprights. Place them 3 inches from the top and bottom and in the middle on the opposite side to give reverse tension.

8 Fasten the stabilizer 1x2s with 1½-inch flathead screws. Position them on the back as shown in the drawing.

Materials: For the shelf unit as shown, you'll need 42 lineal feet of 1x8s, 28 lineal feet of 1x12s, 8 lineal feet of 1x2s, and nine suitcase latches.

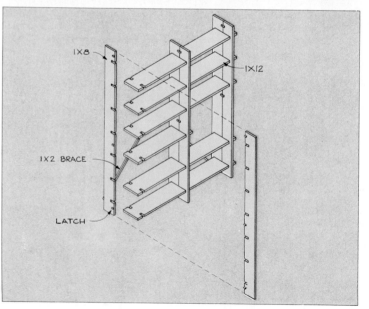

HANDSOME SEE-THROUGH DIVIDER

This stylish project is a great entertainment/activity center and is well worth all the building effort.

1 Plan out the size you want as your first step. Here, the divider is 4½ feet wide, 5½ feet tall, and 14 inches deep.

2 Start by building the base like a five-sided box with the two end pieces extending the full height of the unit.

3 Install the vertical member and the horizontal shelves in the interior of the 'box'.

4 For the upper part, build a 24-inch-high, four-sided box to fit between the two extended ends.

5 (Optional) Apply the decorative panels to both sides, top, and bottom of the unit. Cut these 1½ inches smaller than both dimensions to get the ¾-inch exposure all the way around.

6 Cut the two feet from 4x4s and screw to the bottom.

7 Cut and install the flush doors. Use knife hinges mounted to repeat the design of the sides.

8 Install brackets for the glass shelf in the upper cabinet, and mount track to receive the sliding doors. Mount the track ¾-inch from the cabinet edge, then cut and install the 1x2 trim in front of the tracks. Add the vertical brace.

9 Have glass cut to size (plan a 1-inch overlap for the doors); have your dealer grind the edges.

Materials: For this project, you'll need six sheets ¾-inch plywood, 32 lineal feet 1x2s, 1 lineal foot 4x4, glass doors and shelf, door hardware, and sliding door track.

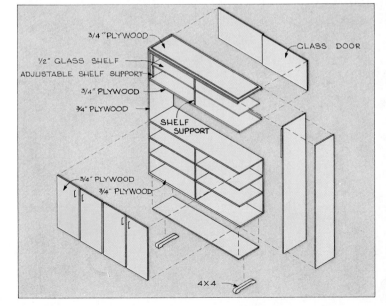

3/4" PLYWOOD

½" GLASS SHELF

ADJUSTABLE SHELF SUPPORT

3/4" PLYWOOD

3/4" PLYWOOD

GLASS DOOR

SHELF SUPPORT

3/4" PLYWOOD

3/4" PLYWOOD

4X4

GARAGE/ BASEMENT

Opportunities for extra storage abound in most every basement or garage. The space is there, ready and waiting to be used, but how you use it can make a world of difference in both capacity and convenience. This chapter's projects show you just how to go about making the most of those opportunities. Both large and small, these units will help organize everything from scrap wood to sports equipment. And, in between, you'll find projects that are planned to store the assortment of bulky things that every family seems to accumulate over the years.

You'll also note that several of the projects in this chapter are planned to function efficiently in either the garage or the basement. So if you spot one that will fill the bill for your family, look to both parts of your house for a place to install it. Better yet, you'll find it's just as easy to build a couple of the smaller projects to install in both locations. So, take that pile of stuff you've got stacked in the corner or jammed into closets around the house and turn it loose on the functional projects in this chapter.

UNIVERSAL UNDER-STAIR STOREHOUSE

This bank of storage capitalizes on every cubic inch of that space under the stairway, and it holds almost anything you need to put away. You may need to alter the individual parts to fit the slope of your stair, but our steps tell you how to build the three basic components. Just fit them to the space you have available.

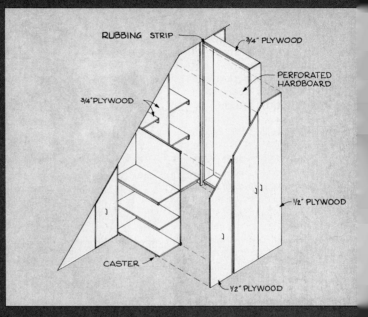

RUBBING STRIP

3/4" PLYWOOD

PERFORATED HARDBOARD

3/4" PLYWOOD

1/2" PLYWOOD

CASTER

1/2" PLYWOOD

1 Work from left to right, beginning with the 20-inch-wide triangular piece at bottom of steps. Cut it to fit, and toenail in place.

2 Build the first and then the second of the roll-out, slant-topped bins. Make the front and back 12 inches wide and ½ inch shorter than the vertical measurement. Cut the tall side from perforated hardboard and shelves from ¾-inch plywood then assemble with butt joints. Recess the lower shelf to allow for the casters you buy. Add a 1x2 rubbing strip to the back of the tall side and the exposed edge of the top shelf so the bins roll easily.

3 Plan the width of the closet unit. Here, it's 3 feet, but it could be narrower. For the enclosure, cut the sides to the height that will fit under the stair, and add a back of

½-inch plywood, cut to fit. Complete the basic box by adding plywood for the "floor" supported with two 1x2s. Install a center divider if closet is more than 2 feet wide, and attach shelves. Nail a 1x2 to edge of each side to create a frame; cut doors to fit and hang with butt hinges.

4 Build the two vertical roll-outs like giant five-sided boxes. Those shown are 7 inches wide. Recess bottom and install platform casters, then add a ½-inch-thick rubbing strip to top and bottom.

Materials: For this project, you'll need five sheets of ¾-inch plywood, one sheet of ½-inch plywood, 12 lineal feet 1x2s, sixteen casters, five hinges, and six large heavy-duty handles.

CORNER CLUTTER CATCHALL

Whether it's your garage or basement, one corner always seems to collect a stack of storables. This organizer not only increases your corner's capacity, it makes every item from trunks to tires handy.

1 Use your box-building skills in a big way on this project. Build the left part 7 feet high, 4 feet wide, and 2 feet deep. Use ¾-inch plywood in an inexpensive grade if you're planning strictly utilitarian storage. Use butt joints and assemble with glue and finishing nails. The cutout on the corner should be 6 inches deep. Add the middle vertical divider at the center and place the shelves 4 feet high.

2 Build the other unit 12 inches deep and 2 feet wide for the best use of your plywood. Divide up the interior spaces as shown—or plan them to fit any special needs. Either way, be sure to work in small niches like these, because you're certain to need them.

3 Enclose the upper part with perforated hardboard doors. Build two 1x2 frames to fit the opening and attach 1x3-foot pieces of ⅛- or ¼-inch hardboard. Install with butt hinges (see page 93).

4 (Optional) For bases, cut two 2x4s for both cabinets if the floor is subject to dampness or if the floor slopes. Drive shims under 2x4 bases to level cabinets.

Materials: For this size project, you'll need five sheets of ¾-inch plywood, 16 lineal feet of 1x2s, a 2x3 piece of perforated hardboard, and two pairs of hinges.

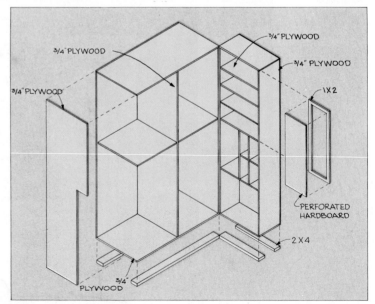

¾" PLYWOOD
¾" PLYWOOD
¾" PLYWOOD
¾" PLYWOOD
1X2
PERFORATED HARDBOARD
2 X 4
¾" PLYWOOD

AN EXTRA OFF-SEASON CLOSET

A good project for the house with sagging closet poles, this swing-open storage unit makes good use of space in your basement. The cedar lining pampers your clothes, and it's a simple matter to switch your wardrobe twice a year.

1 Build the stationary part first. Use ¾-inch plywood for the back, sides, top, and bottom. Here, it's 3½ feet wide, 2 feet deep, and 70 inches tall.

2 Build the hinged section 10 inches deep, with the other dimensions matching those above.

3 Line both boxes with cedar. Lumberyards offer this wood in various ways, including pre-packaged amounts. Either way, just nail it to the insides of both sections, butting the joints and cutting to length as you go.

4 Install the pole and ¾-inch plywood shelves. Center the pole about a foot from the top.

5 Nail 1x2 trim to the front edges of both sections and hang the two small doors.

6 Build a base for the larger unit from 2x4s on edge, and recess it 2 inches from each end. Buy a heavy-duty caster to match the height of the base and attach it.

7 To join the two parts, lay them on the floor in closed position and install piano hinge on outside.

Materials: For the project as shown, you'll need five sheets of ¾-inch plywood, approximately 90 square feet of cedar lining, 38 lineal feet of 1x2s, 10 lineal feet of 2x4s, four butt hinges, one 5-foot piano hinge, and one caster.

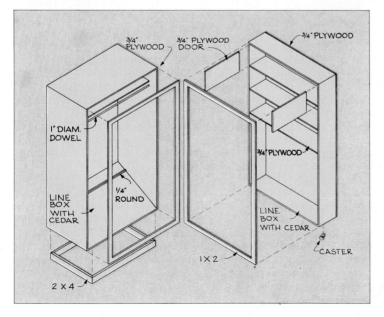

TUCKAWAY GARAGE STORAGE

This two-part project was planned especially for basement garages and takes advantage of space that all too often goes wasted. The king-size drawer slips under the stairs on the other side of the wall, and the storage above uses space within the wall. You can adapt this project to anywhere you need storage in a room adjacent to an under-stair space.

1 The first step is to choose the spot where you can install the drawer. Locate the wall studs and determine which two between-stud spaces you can use.

2 Remove the wall covering material on the near side. If it's paneling like this, gently pry the boards off. For plasterboard, make cutouts with a saber saw, working carefully to come as close to the studs as possible without damaging any of the adjoining areas.

3 To construct the drawer opening, cut the middle stud and toenail two 2x4s across the top of the opening as shown in the drawing. These will provide the necessary support for the stud you cut. It's also a good idea to reinforce that stud above the drawer by nailing another 2x4 to it.

4 Use ¾-inch plywood to construct the drawer according to the dimensions you've worked out. If there's a surface on the other side of the studs, you'll need to remove it, of course, too.

5 To ensure easy operation of the drawer, you'll want to install a framework around the inside of the opening. Use short lengths of 2x4s top and bottom, with ¾-inch plywood sides. The sides will give you a good support for heavy-duty drawer glides (see page 92).

6 For the shallow upper part of this storage unit, install 1x4 shelves between two of the wall studs with shelf support strips or small ledgers. For the other side, nail a 1-inch-thick furring strip around the back corners of the opening, then cut and install a piece of ⅛-inch-thick perforated

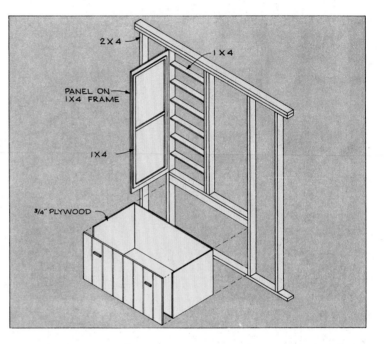

hardboard as pictured.

7 Build the doors to fit the upper opening. Use a framework of 1x4s sized slightly smaller than the opening, as was done here. Cover this framework with the paneling you've salvaged from the opening. Hang the doors with butt hinges and install catches (see page 93).

8 Apply paneling to the drawer front (see false fronts, page 92) and to the horizontal strip between the two parts of the storage project.

Alternate: If your existing wall surface is plasterboard, you'll need to finish off the project differently than in the steps above. Frame both openings with 1x4s nailed in place so that the front edges are flush with the wall surface. For the two doors, use ¾-inch plywood, cut to fit for flush installation (see page 93). For the drawer front, use the same material, cut to allow a ⅛-inch space all the way around the opening. To cover the horizontal support, you can patch in a new piece of plasterboard or cover it with plywood, too.

Materials: To build the project as shown here, you'll need one sheet of ¾-inch plywood, 24 lineal feet of 2x4s, 34 lineal feet of 1x4s, two pairs of hinges, one set of heavy-duty drawer glides, a 16x60-inch piece of perforated hardboard, and 32 square feet of paneling (optional).

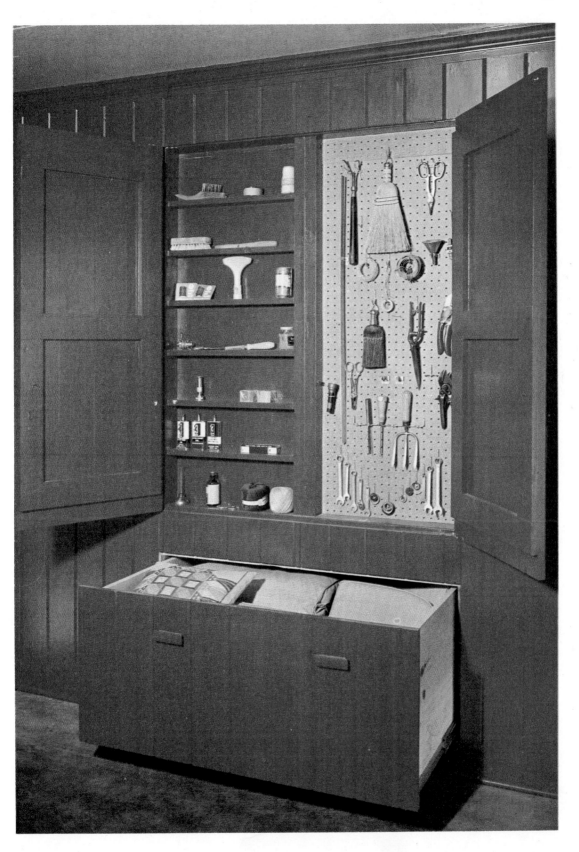

OVERHEAD ODDS 'N ENDS ORGANIZER

Build this handy catchall and in nothing flat you'll have a great spot for narrow pieces of scrap wood, short lengths of piping, and all those other things that collect around a workshop. It's **a good bet that if you build one for the basement, you'll soon build another for the garage—it's handy in either place. And, building two is no problem since it's easy and inexpensive.**

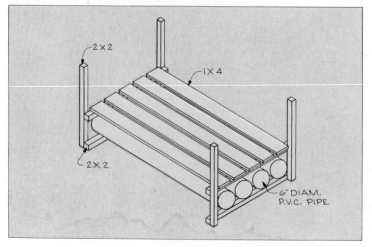

1 Cut the 2x2s and build the two frames first. Here the uprights are 2 feet long and the crosspieces are 28 inches long. Nail and glue them together with lap joints (see page 85).

2 For the upper shelf, nail on five 1x4s, spaced equally in the opening. Or use any scrap wood or plywood that will fit the dimensions of the framework.

3 Cut the four tubes and simply slide them in place. These are 6-inch-diameter PVC pipes, cut to the 4-foot length. Buy this pipe in plumbing shops or departments—it's manufactured for use as large drain piping. You can cut it with any fine-tooth saw. Glue them together or just make sure they fit snugly in the frame. Once they're loaded, you won't have to worry about stability.

4 With a helper, nail the vertical members of the framework to the ceiling joists. The 4-foot length will span four standard-spaced joists when nailed up as shown. If you want to hang your unit so that it parallels the joists, you'll have to adjust the width of the framework, or attach two 2x2s to the bottoms of the joists and nail the framework to them.

5 Use this same construction for more specialized storage such as ski equipment by varying sizes to fit your needs. The PVC pipe is available in several lengths and diameters.

Materials: For the size project shown, you'll need 16 lineal feet of 6-inch diameter PVC drain pipe, 28 lineal feet of 2x2s, and 20 lineal feet of 1x4s.

REC ROOM STORAGE AND SEATING

What basement recreation room has enough storage? And what room like this can't use a little more seating capacity? This easily built project fills both needs and does it in style.

The storage is in the large, underseat "drawers." They're really roll-out bins that can hold a whole floor-full of toys. And, because they're on casters, they make picking up a snap.

1 Cut and assemble the sides of the three separate bases. Use ¾-inch plywood and make them 14 inches high. The corner unit is a 2-foot-square box. The single base is 30 inches wide and the longer one extends 5 feet.

2 Add the center divider in the larger base and then nail 1x4s to all the front edges as shown.

3 Cut the ¾-inch plywood tops for the two seating units and attach with glue and finishing nails.

4 Build a 2-foot square of 1x2s on edge to fit over the corner unit and nail it to the plywood edges. For the removable top, frame a piece of ¾-inch plywood with 1x2s. Miter joints here will pay off in neat appearance. The top isn't attached—just lift it off for access to the space beneath.

5 Measure the openings and build the three bins to fit. Be sure to include the casters in measuring the height. Assemble back, sides, and bottom of each bin, and attach platform casters. Lastly, cut the fronts to clear floor by ½ inch and nail in place.

6 The three sections of your project will be heavy enough to just set into place in most instances. But if you'd like to anchor them together, drill holes through the two ends adjoining the corner unit and attach them with bolts and wing nuts. This way, they are easily disassembled for moving.

Materials: To build the three-part project in the dimensions shown, you'll need two sheets of ¾-inch plywood, 1½ sheets of ½-inch plywood, 8 lineal feet of 1x2s, 6 lineal feet 1x4s, and 12 casters.

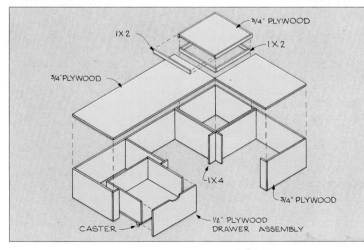

1 X 2
¾" PLYWOOD
1 X 2
¾" PLYWOOD
1 X 4
¾" PLYWOOD
CASTER
½" PLYWOOD DRAWER ASSEMBLY

DRESSY COUNTER STORAGE

Build this low, long, wide, and handsome counter to spark up a dull family room. It offers plenty of convenient storage, and—as a television stand, for instance—it can become the **focal point of your room's furniture arrangement. Position it on an end wall or use our instructions for an alternate arrangement that lets you use the counter to divide a room.**

1 Take the necessary time at the beginning to carefully plan out the desired size for your unit. You can make it wall-to-wall, or allow some flanking space on each end. Note that the end section at the right is planned to be abutted by furniture. You may want to plan one like it on both ends to accommodate your furniture arrangement. The unit shown here is 36 inches high, 24 inches deep, and 11 feet long.

2 Build the end section 2 feet wide with ¾-inch plywood sides, shelves, and dummy front. Assemble with butt joints. The shelves need be only 12 inches deep; cut and install the ¼-inch hardboard divider behind them. Set this unit in place.

3 Next build the base for the remainder of the unit. It's a four-sided frame of 1x4s on edge. Make your frame 22 inches deep to allow for toe space, and as long as you want the counter to be.

4 Build the next section 2 feet wide. Cut the sides and bottom and assemble like a large U, then install the plywood shelf and hardboard backer. Cut plywood doors so they can be recessed in the lower opening and hang them with pivot hinges (see page 93). Set this section in place and for extra stability, secure to end section by screwing through the side into the other one.

5 Continue to build one section at a time. It's a good idea to choose one section for a width adjustment so you can make the completed counter to the exact length you want. Here it's the second section from the left end, which is

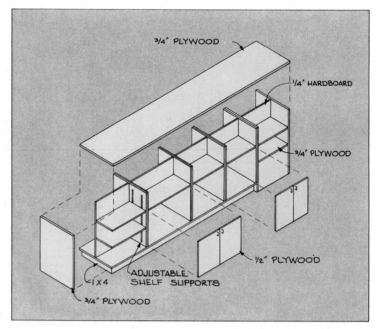

3 feet wide and fills out the 11-foot length exactly. Build the other sections, set them in place, then build this last unit to fit exactly the space left.

Alternate: If you plan your counter to be used as a room divider instead of against a wall, make all the shelves the full 24-inch depth so they'll be accessible from both sides. You can include the hardboard dividers or omit them if you like. For the lower compartments, you can plan solid inset backs, or for easy accessibility, install doors both front and back.

6 Attach support strips in left end section as shown if you want these shelves to be adjustable.

7 Cut the plywood countertop pieces 24 inches wide. If you've

built the counter longer than 8 feet, you'll need two pieces; plan the joint to fall at the point where two of the sections meet. This way, you'll have a solid support for the joint. Nail down the countertop to the storage sections using finishing nails countersunk into the surface.

8 Apply plastic laminate to the top surface and exposed edge with contact cement.

Materials: To build the project as shown, you'll need four sheets of ¾-inch plywood, ½ sheet ½-inch plywood, one sheet of ¼-inch hardboard, 26 lineal feet of 1x4s, 22 square feet of plastic laminate, four pairs of pivot hinges, shelf strips, clips, and four door pulls.

A SYSTEM FOR ALL THAT BULK

Unload all of your bulky storage problems on this basement shelf unit and you'll never have to worry about storing anything heavy or oversize again. The unit proves especially helpful by accommodating suitcases, trunks, lumber, fireplace logs, bricks, and large boxes. Measure the available basement space and adjust the unit to fit that size, but make sure shelves are tall enough to handle specific large items.

1 Lay the three back uprights on the floor; glue and nail three 2x4-inch ledgers and a 2x4-inch base piece to the uprights.
2 Prefab an identical unit by using the three middle uprights and turn it over on the floor. Glue and nail three 2x4-inch ledgers to the other side.
3 Make a third unit using the three front uprights but keep them on edge as you nail the 2x4-inch ledgers to them.
4 Stand the units in place one at a time. Mark the joists and nail 2x2-inch crosspieces to them. Cut shelf pieces from any one-inch lumber.
5 Assemble the unit by anchoring the back section to the joist crosspieces. Locate and anchor the midsection using shelf pieces as spacers. Do the same with the front section. Glue and nail remaining shelves.

Materials: For a 6-foot-long bulk storage unit, you'll need 146 lineal feet of 2x4s, 24 feet of 1x12s, and—for the wide shelves—135 lineal feet of 1x4s or the equivalent.

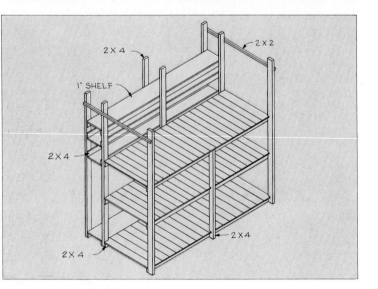

COULDN'T-BE-SIMPLER SHELVES

These basement shelves prove that you don't have to spend a lot of time on a project to get a lot of use from it. In fact, this shelf unit goes up so fast, you might want to build two or three of them to take care of bulk storage problems once and for all. And the shelves are just as handy in the garage as they are in the basement; build them the same way and nail to joists, rafters, or crossties. Since you're building this project for function rather than appearance, use lower grades of lumber, or scrap if you have it.

1 Cut two vertical 2x4s to a length that will allow 3 inches overlap for nailing. Plan a spot for the shelves and measure the distance from the outside of one 2x4 to the outside of the other.

2 Use this dimension for the length of the 1x4 shelf supports. Cut the 1x4s and nail them to the edges of both 2x4s, spaced to fit the items you want to store.

3 Swing the framework into place and plumb the 2x4s with a level, marking the location on the ceiling joists above. Then just nail the 2x4s to the joists.

4 Then cut the 1x12 shelves to fit between the 2x4s; center each shelf over the 1x4s, and nail it in place. NOTE: If you build two or more parallel shelf units, allow at least 2 feet between them for access space.

Materials: For a single 4-foot-long shelf unit, you'll need 16 feet of 2x4s, 32 lineal feet of 1x4s, and 16 lineal feet of 1x12s.

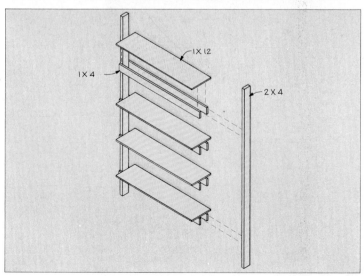

SPECIAL-PURPOSE STORAGE

Every family has interests and activities that create special needs. Some of these needs are centered around the whole family, while others involve only one member. The projects here were chosen especially to help you solve those unique storage problems connected with these activities. You may even find one or two that will encourage you to organize an activity that's now so dispersed around your house it creates a real storage crunch.

Several of the designs you'll find in this chapter can fit in many different rooms of your house. So pick out the projects you know you can use, then find the right location for them—and be creative as you plan. The home office on these pages, for instance, can work just as well in a bedroom as it would in a kitchen or family room. Check your house for spaces that aren't used to their fullest. A hallway, stair landing, or entryway can often yield a spot big enough for one of the projects in this chapter.

And, once you've found the project and the place, the rest is as easy as one, two, three.

27

ALL-PURPOSE HOME OFFICE

This compact office will help any family get organized. It offers enough storage to be used as a family business center, then converts for one of the kids' homework. And you can install an optional cover-up—a window shade attached to the natural-finished 1x4 just below the top shelf.

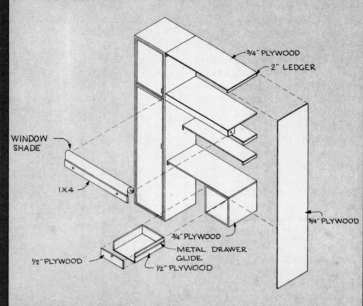

3/4" PLYWOOD
2" LEDGER
WINDOW SHADE
1X4
1/2" PLYWOOD
3/4" PLYWOOD
METAL DRAWER GLIDE
1/2" PLYWOOD
3/4" PLYWOOD

1 Build the tall storage cabinet on the left first. Use ¾-inch plywood with butt joints and make the overall box 18 inches square and 7 feet high. Add the horizontal divider at a height of 5 feet.
2 Cut the cabinet doors and install with butt hinges. Trim with screen bead molding, if you like.
3 Cut 7-foot by 18-inch right end support and nail it into a corner as shown in photograph.
4 Make the two upper shelves the full 18-inch depth of your office, and the other shelves and work surface 16 inches deep. You can adjust the width, but don't make it much narrower than the 36 inches here. Install all four shelves and work surface with ledger strips.
5 Build a four-sided, 14-inch

square box for the drawers and attach it to the bottom of the desk surface with screws, then install the two parts with ledger strips.
6 Build the two drawers and install with metal drawer glides (see page 92).
7 Add a 1x4 trim board to the shelf to conceal the window shade. Then get a shade cut to fit the opening and install it. Lastly, add the other 1x4 to the shade as a pull if you like.

Materials: For the project as shown, you'll need four sheets of ¾-inch plywood, 6 lineal feet of 1x4s, 20 lineal feet of screen bead molding (optional), two pairs of drawer glides, and the optional window shade.

BOX-IN PROBLEM ITEMS

Besides being a good practical way of storing excess clutter, this throw-it-in-a-box storage idea is a great way to liven up a blank wall. It also proves that good storage needn't always be out of sight, out of mind. Mostly just a matter of assembly, this is a project you can accomplish with just two tools—a drill and a screwdriver.

1 Attach the two shelf standards to the wall. Use 6-footers and space them to fit the shortest box you plan to use. You can drive the screws into the wall studs, if the location is right. Or, choose another of the wall-hanging methods shown on page 90.

2 Scout around for a source of boxes similar to these. Most retail stores will sell boxes they regularly package their wares in. To get the effect shown here, buy a coordinated assortment of paint in spray cans and spray the outside surfaces of the boxes.

3 For the tell-tale labels, buy press-on letters at an art supply store and spell out the contents of each box. The lettering adds to the overall effect and saves you searching through the boxes later.

4 Install the shelf brackets to hold each box. Slip the hooks into slots in the standards and tap each lightly to make them fit snugly.

Materials: For the project as shown, you'll need two 6-foot-long shelf standards, sixteen 12-inch brackets, and, of course, the boxes. The larger ones here are 30x14x5 inches; the smaller ones are 18 inches wide.

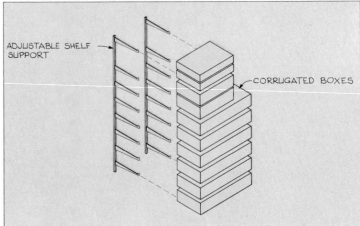

ADJUSTABLE SHELF SUPPORT

CORRUGATED BOXES

HANDY
DESK-TOP
CATCHALL

This project is small in both the material and the effort required to build it. But the catchall packs a real wallop in organizing pencils, papers, cards, and even little things like paper clips and stamps. You can apply a finish to match your desk, or go with a bright color to give your work area new life.

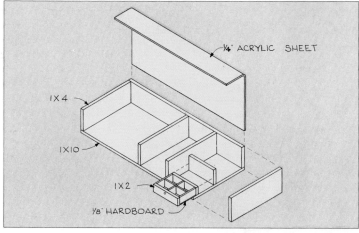

1 Start by cutting the bottom of the catchall from a 1x10. Here, it's 29 inches long. Choose a top grade of pine for appearance.

2 Use 1x4s for the back, ends, and the two dividers. Assemble with butt joints, applying glue and nailing through the bottom into the 1x4s. Countersink the finishing nails. NOTE: You can space the dividers to suit yourself, but it's a good idea to make the larger space 11¼ inches wide to accommodate standard stationery.

3 Cut the other small divider and glue it in place—a snug fit will eliminate nailing. Make the small slide-out box from scraps you have.

4 For the plastic dust cover, choose ¼-inch-thick acrylic sheet (here, it's smoke color). Cut it to the same length as the back with a saw or a special inexpensive cutting tool. For the width, add the depth and height of your catchall and cut to that dimension. Polish the edges of the cover at this point.

5 Mark the line for the bend in the cover and heat that line with an electric strip heater made for that purpose. These are available where you buy the acrylic sheet. When pliable, just bend the corner and hold it in place until the plastic cools.

6 Attach cover with strap hinges bolted to the cover and screwed into the back.

Materials: For the project as shown, you'll need 3 lineal feet of 1x10 lumber, 7 lineal feet of 1x4s, acrylic sheet, and two strap hinges.

A PLACE FOR TOOLS—PLUS WORKBENCH

You can build this rollabout to hold all the tools in the house—and then add the work surface that makes it into a mobile workbench. Build it as shown here, or alter the number of drawers (or their size) to fit your equipment exactly.

1 For base, mount platform casters (two with locks) on 30x30-inch piece of ¾-inch plywood.

2 Then build two 15x30-inch boxes for the drawers—but make one of them without a top and join them with a common 30x30-inch back. Add the center dividers.

3 Saw another 30x30-inch piece of plywood for the back side and attach it with a 15x30-inch divider in the middle. Then nail on the 30x30-inch top.

4 Nail on base from bottom and outfit insides with drawers (see page 92) and shelves.

5 Build a four-sided 18x18x6-inch box for the top and nail in the center. Then build a simple drawer that you can open from either end.

6 Then add the work surface on top. It's also 30 inches square and made from ¾-inch plywood.

7 Finish off the project by adding the electrical outlet with a heavy-duty extension cord, a small vise, a towel holder, and hooks for hanging large tools on the sides.

Materials: To build the unit as shown, you'll need two sheets of ¾-inch plywood, 1½ sheets of ½-inch plywood, eight pairs of drawer glides, four platform casters, and (optional) outlet, lamp, vise, hooks, and towel holder.

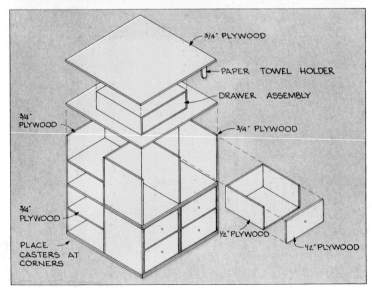

Here's the spot for the harvest from your garden. Each shelf will hold either 77 pint jars or 56 quarts. And, you can easily add another module of either height if you need it.

1 Cut 2 feet off three sheets of ¾-inch plywood and then saw the 4x6-foot pieces into four 2x3-foot shelves.

2 From the 2x4 pieces remaining, saw two more shelves (one for the 37½-inch-wide countertop).

3 From the rest of the plywood, cut the four 3-inch-wide bottom shelf supports and the other 2-inch supports.

4 Next build the two "ladder" ends for the taller side with four 78-inch 2x4s. Space the shelf supports every 8¾ inches.

5 Stand the "ladders" on edge and temporarily nail on a scrap piece to steady them. Nail in the bottom, top, and one middle shelf (other shelves are removable).

6 Remove the temporary holder and turn the unit facedown on the floor. Nail a diagonal 1x4 brace to the back, driving nails into both 2x4s and all three shelves. (Or, enclose the back with ⅛-inch hardboard.) Lift into place.

7 To add the shorter section, build a 36-inch-long ladder, add supports for the attached end, and connect by nailing two shelves and the top.

8 Slip the remaining shelves into place on the shelf supports.

Materials: For the project as shown, you'll need three sheets of ¾-inch plywood and 32 lineal feet of 2x4s.

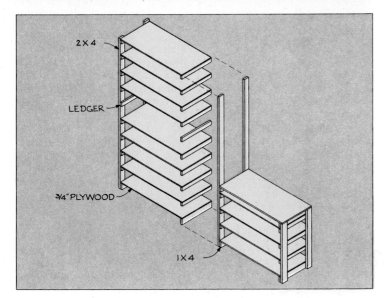

HALLWAY TURNED LIBRARY

These bookshelves are simple and straightforward, but look at the soaring storage they provide in an otherwise useless hallway. Use this idea in most any space where traffic is channeled along the wall and there's not enough floor space for furniture. You can alter the widths to fit the area you have and load the shelves with books and accessories.

1 Work out the widths of the bookcases first. Here the 10-foot-wide wall space is divided into five 2-foot sections. But you could make the spaces between the three units a different width instead of dividing them equally. Either way, once you've established the size you want, the rest is easy.

2 Cut the verticals about an inch shorter than your floor-to-ceiling measurement to allow room to tilt the bookcase up in place. All the wood in this project is 1x8. If you choose another depth, be sure to experiment with the "swing up" allowance before you start building the project

3 Notch out the necessary space for the baseboard and base shoe moldings, if necessary. You can cut a cardboard pattern, then trace it on each vertical and cut the notch with a coping saw.

4 Next cut the 2-foot-long bookshelves as uniformly as possible and plan the shelf spacing in each of the three bookcases. No need to make them all alike; you'll do better by planning certain shelves for certain books (but don't squeeze the space too closely; you'll need finger room to remove the volumes).

5 Saw dadoes for the shelves on the insides of the vertical members and plan a rabbet joint at the top (see page 86).

6 Assemble the three bookcases with white glue and either finishing nails or flat-headed wood screws countersunk into the outside surfaces.

7 Attach the full-height lengths of shelf strips at this point. The work

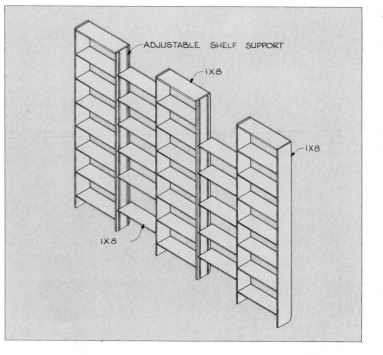

will go a lot faster if you lay the bookcases first on one side and then the other to drive the screws.

8 Swing the units upright and slide them to get the two "in between" spaces equal. Tall bookcases of this type will generally be stable, but it's smart to anchor them to the wall to prevent accidental tipping. Screw two small corner angles to the inside of the bookcases in an inconspicuous spot and then drive screws into the wall studs.

9 Cut and install the two tiers of shelves between the bookcases. It's easiest to cut them to fit between the strips. Or, for a neater installation, cut them to a length

that will let the shelves fit loosely between the outsides of the bookcases. Then, saw shallow dadoes in both ends of the shelves to allow for the shelf strips.

10 Snap the clips into the shelf support brackets (most of them have numbers on the notches to help you place the clips correctly) and place the shelves wherever they work best for the things you want to display.

Materials: For the complete project as shown, you'll need 118 lineal feet of 1x8s, 64 lineal feet of shelf-support strips, and shelf clips.

STUD SPACE PUT TO GOOD USE

Any and every wall in your house has this kind of storage space lurking inside. All you have to do is cut an access to it and outfit the space with the kind of shelves you need. Our steps show you how to build one of the units pictured. You can eliminate cutting a stud (step 3) if you plan your unit to fit between two adjoining studs.

1 Locate the studs in the wall you want to use (see page 90) and then check to see if wiring or pipes are concealed inside by checking the location in the basement or attic.

2 Cut away the wallboard between three studs with a saber saw. Follow the inside edges of the studs for vertical lines; draw horizontal lines for the other cuts.

3 Saw the middle stud at the top and bottom of the opening and remove it. Then add horizontal 2x4s top and bottom.

4 Build a frame with 1x4s to match the size of the opening and add a ¼-inch plywood back. Install 1x4 shelves. NOTE: Use 1x6s if you want a deeper cabinet but remember it will project 2 inches into the room.

5 Slip the unit into the opening and fasten with nails through the sides into the wall studs.

6 Cut the door from ¾-inch plywood and attach it to the 1x4 frame with pivot hinges.

Materials: For both units as shown, you'll need ½ sheet of ¼- and ¾-inch plywood, 40 lineal feet of 1x4s, 6 lineal feet 2x4s, and two pairs of hinges.

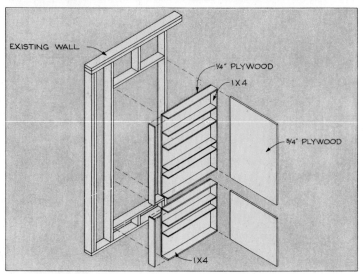

EXISTING WALL

¼" PLYWOOD

1X4

¾" PLYWOOD

1X4

BIG BAR IN A SMALL SPACE

Here's a great way to build a bar where you don't have much room. And, although it looks built-in, it really isn't. You can dismantle it at a moment's notice for redecorating or moving. And, it works just as well against a wall as it does here, placed as a room divider.

1 Measure your floor-to-ceiling height and cut two 4x4 posts 1 inch short of that measurement.

2 Attach shelf support strips of the type used for bookshelves. They need not extend the full height of the posts.

3 Install the posts by attaching adjustable furniture glides top and bottom. These are available in larger hardware stores and are ordinarily used as feet for handmade furniture. Screw them into both ends of the posts far enough so that you can swing the posts into a vertical position. Use a level to make sure you get the posts exactly vertical, and then unscrew the upper glides until they tighten firmly against the ceiling. Measure the distance between them at top and bottom to ensure that they're parallel.

4 Slip shelf brackets in place and then just rest the glass shelves on them. It's easiest to get the shelves cut and edges polished at the glass dealer's (these are 36x12 inches).

Materials: For the project as shown, you'll need 16 lineal feet of 4x4s, 12 lineal feet of shelf standards, 12 brackets, four furniture glides, and six glass shelves.

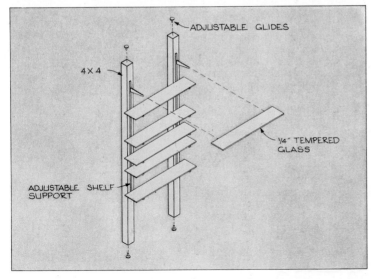

ADJUSTABLE GLIDES

4 X 4

¼" TEMPERED GLASS

ADJUSTABLE SHELF SUPPORT

PLANNING AND BUILDING BASICS

Have you ever heard the saying, "It's not hard once you know how to do it"? Well it's true, especially when it comes to building projects for your home. Once you've mastered the basics, each project you do becomes a series of accomplishable steps rather than a major undertaking.

So, do yourself a favor and spend a few minutes learning about the steppingstones to professional-looking projects. It'll be worth your while.

COMMON CONSTRUCTION MATERIALS

The materials you use for construction will vary, depending on the item's intended use. So when making your selection, ask yourself these questions: Are you constructing something for indoor or outdoor use? Is the item strictly utilitarian, or will it be suitable for use in a living room? Is it intended for light-duty use, or will it be a long-lived project subject to considerable use—and abuse?

Hardboard

Hardboard is available in 4x8-foot sheets and comes in ⅛- and ¼-inch thicknesses. Standard hardboard is an excellent choice for cabinetwork, drawer bottoms, and concealed panels.

You can also get hardboard perforated with holes spaced about one inch apart. Perforated hardboard is recommended for building storage for soiled laundry and for the backs of hi-fi cabinets. The quarter- and eighth-inch perforated hardboard lends itself to storing garden equipment and tools, too, as its holes accept hooks designed for this purpose. To expand or change the arrangement, just switch the hooks around. If the project will be subject to dampness, use tempered hardboard.

Particle board, chip board, and flake board, also members of the hardboard family, have a coarser grain structure, are lighter in color, and are available in thicknesses up to ¾ inch. These products are made of granulated or shredded wood particles forced together under pressure with a binder at high temperatures.

Plywood

Plywood also comes in 4x8-foot sheets, though larger sheets are available on special order. Thicknesses range from ⅛-inch to ¾-inch. For light-duty storage, the ¼- and ½-inch thicknesses are adequate. If you are planning to build an outdoor storage unit, specify *exterior grade* when making your purchase. Exterior grade plywood has its layers glued together with a waterproof glue to withstand rain.

The surfaces of plywood sheets are graded A, B, C, and D—with A the smoother, better surface and D the least desirable appearance. Choose AA (top grade, both sides) only for projects where both sides will be exposed; use a less expensive combination for others.

Solid Wood

Plain, ordinary wood still ranks as the most popular building material. Wood is sold by the "board foot" (1x12x12 inches). One board foot equals the surface area of one square foot, with a nominal thickness of one inch.

Wood is marketed by "grade." For most building projects No. 2 grade will satisfy your needs. This grade may have some blemishes, such as loose knots, but these don't reduce the strength of the wood.

If you're planning to build a unit that will be part of a room's decor, you should buy *select lumber*—a grade that's relatively free of blemishes.

Remember, too, that outdoor projects are a different subject. Redwood or cedar is preferable, but if you use a soft wood such as fir, be sure to treat it for moisture resistance.

You can buy boards up to 16 feet in length and 12 inches in width, though occasionally a lumberyard may have somewhat wider or longer boards.

Wood is divided into two categories. Softwoods, used commonly for general construction, come from trees that don't shed their leaves in the winter: hemlock, fir, pine, spruce, and similar evergreen cone-bearing trees. Hardwoods come from trees that do shed their leaves: maple, oak, birch, mahogany, walnut, and other broad-leaved varieties.

All lumber is sold by a nominal size. A 2x4, for example, does not measure two by four inches. It's actually 1½x3½ inches (though the nominal *length* of a 2x4 is usually its true length). The drawing shows nominal sizes, as well as the actual sizes, of most pieces of common lumber.

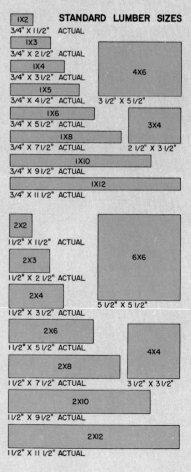

STANDARD LUMBER SIZES

1X2 — 3/4" X 1 1/2" ACTUAL
1X3 — 3/4" X 2 1/2" ACTUAL
1X4 — 3/4" X 3 1/2" ACTUAL
1X5 — 3/4" X 4 1/2" ACTUAL
1X6 — 3/4" X 5 1/2" ACTUAL
1X8 — 3/4" X 7 1/2" ACTUAL
1X10 — 3/4" X 9 1/2" ACTUAL
1X12 — 3/4" X 11 1/2" ACTUAL
4X6 — 3 1/2" X 5 1/2"
3X4 — 2 1/2" X 3 1/2"
2X2 — 1 1/2" X 1 1/2" ACTUAL
2X3 — 1 1/2" X 2 1/2" ACTUAL
2X4 — 1 1/2" X 3 1/2" ACTUAL
6X6 — 5 1/2" X 5 1/2"
2X6 — 1 1/2" X 5 1/2" ACTUAL
2X8 — 1 1/2" X 7 1/2" ACTUAL
4X4 — 3 1/2" X 3 1/2"
2X10 — 1 1/2" X 9 1/2" ACTUAL
2X12 — 1 1/2" X 11 1/2" ACTUAL

WOOD JOINTS YOU SHOULD KNOW

No matter what material you're planning to use, it will have to be cut to size—measure twice and cut once is a good rule—then put together using glue, nails or screws, and one of these joints.

Butt Joints

The simplest joint of all, the butt joint, consists of two pieces of wood meeting at a right angle and

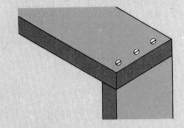

held together with nails, or preferably, screws (see sketch). A dab of glue before using the nails or screws will make the joint even more secure. But don't use glue if you're planning to take the work apart sometime later.

When reinforced by one of the six methods illustrated, the butt joint is effective for making corner

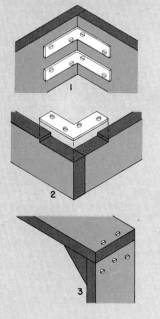

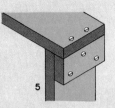

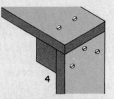

joints. Two common fasteners are angle irons (1), and flat corner plates (2). Using scrap wood, you can reinforce the joint with a triangular wedge (3), or with a square block (4). A variation of the square block places the block on the outside of the joint (5). Finally, a triangular gusset made from plywood or hardboard will also serve to reinforce a corner butt joint (6).

When a butt joint is in the form of a T—for example, in making a framework for light plywood or hardboard—you can reinforce it with an angle iron, T plate, or corrugated fasteners.

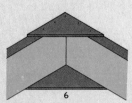

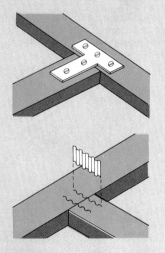

For really rough work, you can drive in a couple of nails at an

angle, or toenail (see sketch). A variation of this is to place a block of wood alongside the crosspiece

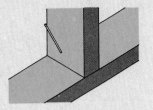

and secure it with a couple of nails.

A close cousin to the T joint and the butt joint is the plain overlap joint. It is held in place with at least two screws (see sketch). For extra reinforcement, apply glue between the pieces of wood.

Butt joints are an excellent means of securing backs to various units, especially when appearance is not a factor. Simply cut the back to the outside di-

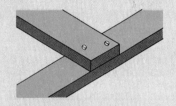

mensions of the work, then nail in place . . . it's called a flush back.

Lap Joints

On those projects where appearance is vital, consider full and half-lap joints. To make a full lap joint, cut a recess in one of the pieces of wood equal in depth to the thickness of the crossmember (see sketch).

The half-lap joint is similar to the full lap joint when finished, but the technique is different. First, cut a recess equal to half the

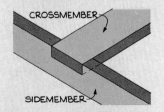

CROSSMEMBER

SIDEMEMBER

thickness of the crossmember halfway through the crossrail. Then, make a similar cut in the opposite half of the other piece (see sketch on the next page).

Butt joints and overlap joints do

not require any extra work besides cutting the pieces to size. However, full and half-lap joints

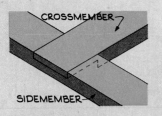

CROSSMEMBER

SIDEMEMBER

require the use of a backsaw and a chisel. For a full-lap joint, mark off the thickness and width of the crossmember on the work in which it is to fit.

Use the backsaw to make a cut at each end that's equal to the thickness of the crossmember, then use a chisel to remove the wood between the backsaw cuts. Check for sufficient depth and finish off with a fine rasp or sandpaper. Apply white glue to the mating surfaces and insert two screws to hold the joint securely.

Dado Joints

The dado joint is a simple way of suspending a shelf from its side supports. To make a dado joint, draw two parallel lines with a knife

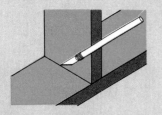

across the face of the work equal to the thickness of the wood it is to engage (see sketch). The depth should be about one-third of the thickness of the wood.

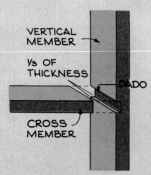

VERTICAL
MEMBER

⅓ OF
THICKNESS

DADO

CROSS
MEMBER

Next, make cuts on these lines and one or more between the lines

with a backsaw. Then, chisel out the wood to the correct depth.

You can speed the job immeasurably by using a router, a bench saw, or a radial arm saw. Any one of these power tools makes the cutting of dadoes an easy job — and provides much greater accuracy than can be achieved by hand.

If appearance is a factor, consider the stopped dado joint. In this type of joint, the dado (the cutaway part) extends only part way, and only a part of the shelf is cut away to match the non-cut part of the dado.

To make a stopped dado, first make your guide marks and chisel away a small area at the stopped end to allow for saw movement. Then make saw cuts

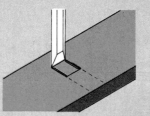

along your guide marks to the proper depth. Next chisel out the waste wood as shown in sketch.

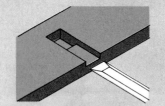

And finally, cut away a corner of the connecting board to accommodate the stopped dado.

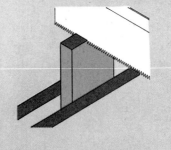

Rabbet Joints

The rabbet joint is really a partial dado. As you can see in the drawing, only one of the meeting members is cut away. It's a simple

joint and, of course, should be secured with nails or screws and glue.

The backs of many units are rabbeted for the best appearance

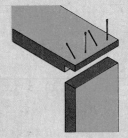

(called inset backs). To make this joint, carefully measure the distance between the rabbeted openings and cut the back accordingly. Then, use thin screws to secure the back to the unit.

Mortise and Tenon Joints

A particularly strong joint, the mortise and tenon joint is excellent when used for making T joints, right-angle joints, and for joints in the middle of rails. As its name indicates, this joint has two parts—the *mortise,* which is the open part of the joint, and the *tenon,* the part that fits into the mortise (see sketch).

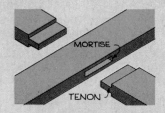

MORTISE

TENON

Make the mortise first, as it is much easier to fit the tenon to the mortise than the other way around. Divide the rail (the part to be mortised) into thirds and carefully mark off the depth and the width of the opening with a sharp pencil.

Next, use a chisel, equal to the width of the mortise, to remove the wood between the pencil marks. You can expedite this job by drilling a series of holes in the rail with an electric drill, a drill press, or even a hand drill. (If you have a drill press, you can purchase a special mortising bit that will drill square holes, believe it or not.) Mark the drill bit with a bit of tape to indicate the desired depth. Now use the chisel to remove the excess wood.

To make the tenon, divide the rail into thirds, mark the required depth, and use a backsaw to remove unwanted wood. If you have a bench or radial saw, the job of removing the wood will be much easier. Use a dado blade and set the blades high enough to remove the outer third of the wood. Reverse the work and remove the lower third, leaving the inner third intact.

To assemble, make a trial fit, and if all is well, apply some white glue to the tenon and insert it into the mortise. If by chance the tenon is too small for the mortise, simply insert hardwood wedges at top and bottom.

Use moderate clamping pressure on the joint until the glue dries overnight. Too much pressure will squeeze out the glue, actually weakening the joint.

Miter Joints

You can join two pieces of wood meeting at a right angle rather elegantly with a miter joint. And it's not a difficult joint to make. All you need is a miter box and a backsaw, or a power saw that you can adjust to cut at a 45 degree angle.

Since the simple miter joint is a surface joint with no shoulders for support, you must reinforce it. The easiest way to do this is with nails and glue (see sketch). You'll notice that most picture frames are made this way.

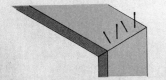

However, for cabinet and furniture work, you may use other means of reinforcement. One way is to use a hardwood spline as shown in the drawing. Apply glue to the spline and to the mitered

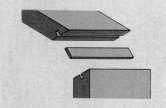

area and clamp as shown until the glue dries.

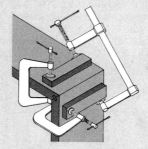

A variation of the long spline uses several short splines—at least three—inserted at opposing angles.

Dowels are a popular method of reinforcing a mitered joint, too. Careful drilling of the holes is necessary to make certain the dowel holes align. Use dowels that are slightly shorter than the holes they are to enter to allow for glue at the bottom. Score or roughen the

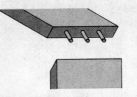

dowels to give the glue a better surface for a strong bond.

Dovetail Joints

The dovetail joint is a sign of good craftsmanship. It's a strong joint especially good for work subject to heavy loads.

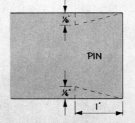

To make the joint, first draw the outline of the pin as shown and cut away the excess wood with a sharp backsaw. Place the pin over the second piece of wood and draw its outline with a sharp pencil. Make the two side cuts with the backsaw and an additional cut or two to facilitate the next step—chiseling away the excess wood. Then test for fit, apply glue and clamp the pieces until

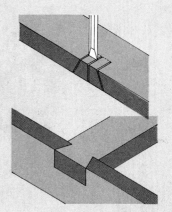

dry. This is the basic way to make most dovetail joints. However, it's much easier to make dovetail joints with a router and dovetail template, especially made for home craftsman use.

Mitered Dovetail Joints

As its name implies, this joint—sometimes called a *secret miter*—combines a miter with a dovetail. It is an exacting joint to make, and like the dovetail joint, a mark of true craftsmanship. The first step is to miter-cut the two pieces of wood to be joined at a 45 degree angle. Then cut away the

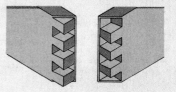

pins and the dovetails as shown. Be careful to make all openings between the pins and dovetails the same depth.

Corner Joints

These joints are used for attaching legs to corners for framing. A good technique for joining corners is the three-way joint involving a set of steel braces you can buy. First, insert the bolt into the inside corner of the leg. Then cut slots into the side members, and secure the brace with two screws at each end. Finally, tighten the wing nut.

A variation of the three-way joint uses dowels and a triangular ¾-inch-thick gusset plate for additional reinforcement. To make this joint, first glue the dowels in

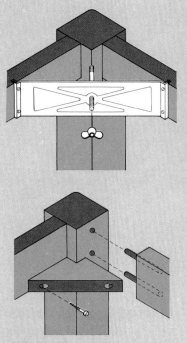

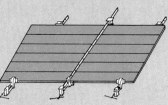

workbench, or a large storage cabinet, this joint fills the bill. To make it, glue together two or more boards, then hold securely with either bar or pipe clamps. If the boards have a pronounced grain, reverse them side-to-side

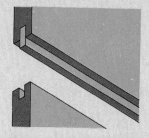

to minimize warping. For additional strength, screw cleats to the underside of the boards.

You also can use hardwood splines to join several boards. Cut a groove the exact width of the spline along the meeting sides of the two boards (see sketch). Cut the grooves slightly deeper than the spline width and in the exact center of the board thickness. The best way to cut such grooves is with a router or a bench saw.

dowels. Score the dowels, apply glue, join the two boards together, and clamp with pipe or bar clamps until the glue sets (allow plenty of time).

If you'll be drilling many dowel holes, you may want to use a wood or metal template to ensure accurate spacing.

Box Joints

One joint is so common in the construction of boxes — and drawers — it's called a *box joint,* or a *finger joint because its parts* look like the outstretched fingers of a hand (see sketch). Note that one of the mating pieces must have two end fingers, or one more

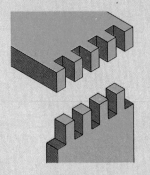

the vertical piece (see sketch). Let them dry completely, then finish the assembly.

A glued miter joint, reinforced with screws and glue, also makes a good corner joint. Make sure the screws do not penetrate the outside surface of the mitered joint.

You can also use a tenon and a dado cut, with screws, to make a good corner joint. Make sure that the holes for the screws are not in line with each other. Use flat-head screws and countersink the holes.

The simplest corner joint of all is a butt joint for the two horizontal members (see sketch). Instead of being fastened to each other,

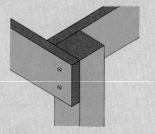

the butted members are each fastened to the corner post with screws.

Edge-to-Edge Joints

Whenever an extra-wide surface is required, such as a desk top,

Then assemble with glue and clamps.

Another possibility for joining several boards involves the use of dowels. To make this joint, first make holes in the boards. You can either use a doweling jig or a drill. If you use a drill, first drive

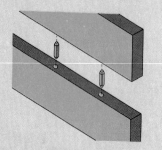

brads (small finishing nails) into one board and press them against the second board to leave marks for drilling. Make the dowel holes slightly deeper than the

finger than the piece it is to engage. You can make this joint by hand with a backsaw and a small, sharp chisel. However, it is much easier, quicker, and more accurate to make it on a bench saw. Use a dado blade set to the desired width and proper depth of the fingers and mark off the waste area so there will be no mistake as to what you want to cut away.

STORAGE UNIT SPECIFICATIONS

A countertop that's too low to work at comfortably, a clothes pole that allows garments to drag, a bookcase that has the wrong height shelves—all are the result of poor planning. The information presented here will help you avoid such pitfalls.

General Considerations

If you're planning to build a bookcase for storing books, don't make the spacing between shelves uniform. Rather, design the shelves progressively closer together from bottom to top. There's no need to stick to an exact uniform progression, however. The same applies to the drawers in a chest.

When designing a vertical unit consisting of two vertical compartments, plan both of equal width. For furniture with three or more compartments, the center compartment(s) should be wider than the end compartments.

When planning a unit with four vertical sections, there are three possibilities, each in good taste. All of the sections can be of equal width; the two central sections can be of equal width with the two end sections narrower; or the two middle sections, still of equal width, can be narrower than the end sections.

Bookcases

It's good to keep these points in mind when planning the internal dimensions of a bookcase. In most cases, the space for large "coffee table" books should measure 11x14½ inches; novels, 7x8 inches; paperbacks, 4½x7 inches; and general magazines, 9x11 inches. Records in display albums measure 12½x14 inches (in standard jackets, 12½x12½ inches,) while 78 rpm records measure 10½x10½ inches, and 45 rpms require 7½x7½ inches for storage. Always allow an extra inch in the vertical direction for comfortable access.

Incidentally, due to the narrow width of paperbacks, you can store two rows on the same shelf, one behind the other. Pack books in the front row loosely so you can shift them to see the titles behind.

Kitchen Cabinets

Kitchen counter cabinets are always 36 inches high, 24 inches deep, and as long as necessary. Cabinets above the countertop are usually 24 to 34 inches high and 12 inches deep, with a filler soffit beteen the top of the cabinets and the ceiling. (They're always of shallower depth than

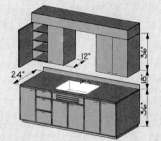

the counter cabinets.) Allow at least 18 inches between the countertop and the storage cabinets above them.

Wardrobes

When building a wardrobe, keep in mind that the clothes pole should be a minimum of 12 inches from the wall. Space permitting, an extra few inches is a good idea, too, because then you can store infrequently used clothes on hooks behind the clothes pole. Store shoes on a raised platform sloping toward the front of the closet with a ½-inch-diameter quarter round bar parallel to the

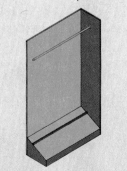

width of the closet. The bar engages the heels of the shoes, preventing them from sliding for-

ward, and makes for neat, economical use of the storage area.

Linen Closets

These should have adjustable shelves, with the deepest one at the bottom. You can use the topmost shelf—the one that is least used because of its height—to store luggage, winter blankets, and other items that are more or less seasonal.

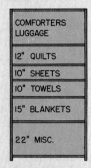

Walk-In Closets

If it's big enough to walk in, it should have shelves on at least one side, two clothes poles, and complete shelving above the clothes poles. Minimum width of a

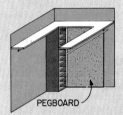

walk-in with clothes poles on both sides is 5 feet, 8 inches. With a pole on only one side, it should be at least 3 feet, 10 inches wide. More is better in both cases.

Reserve one set of shelves for women's shoes. These shelves can be fairly close together—about 4¾ inches, or the height of a shoe box.

The clothes pole height should be at least 72 inches if used for evening gowns or garment bags. For regular garments, 66 inches is sufficient.

For double tier hanging, plan the upper pole at a height of 78 inches above the floor and the lower pole at 36 inches. This system is good for shirts, blouses, pants, and most other shorter items of clothing.

SUPPORT SYSTEMS

Any item you construct, no matter how light, must be capable of supporting itself as well as its "payload". Even a simple box has a support system: its sides are self-supporting, each one serving to support and strengthen its neighbor.

How to Attach Things to Walls

Many items, such as shelves and wall-hung cabinets, depend on the wall as part of their support system. However, you can't always drive a nail or insert a screw just anywhere in a wall. For best stability, drive them into the studs of the wall.

Locating studs. One way of locating wall studs is to rap the wall with your knuckles. Listen for a "solid" sound. (Thumps between the studs will sound hollow.) This works fine if you have excellent hearing.

A far easier way is to buy an inexpensive stud finder. Its magnetic needle will respond to hidden nails, indicating the presence of a stud.

Locating one stud does not necessarily mean that the next stud is 16 inches away, though. It should be, but many times it isn't. For example, if the framework of a door or wall falls 20 inches away from the last stud, the builder may have left a 20-inch gap between them. Or, a stud may have been placed midway, leaving 10-inch spaces on either side.

Fastening to hollow-core walls. Quite often, because of physical requirements, you will need to make an installation between studs into a hollow plaster wall.

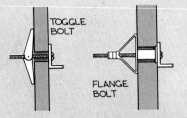

What then? The answer is to use flange or toggle bolts. They distribute their load over a wide area,

and if used in sufficient number and with discretion, they'll hold a fairly heavy load.

Fastening to masonry. Attaching items to a masonry wall is not difficult. if you're working with a brick, concrete, or cinder block wall, use a carbide-tipped drill to make a hole *in the mortar*. Make the hole deep and wide enough to accept a wall plug. Then insert the screw or bolt to fasten the item in place (see sketch).

Another method of fastening to

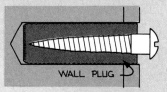

WALL PLUG

masonry walls is to drill a ½-inch hole in the *mortar* and pound a hardwood dowel into the hole. Bevel the end of the dowel and lightly coat it with grease before driving it in place. Then drill a pilot hole in the middle of the dowel and continue with the fastening.

If by chance you must drill into the brick part of a wall rather than the mortar, don't despair. Again use a carbide-tipped drill, but this time start with a ¼-inch bit, and finish with the larger size desired.

How to Mount Units On a Base

If your project is any type of cabinet, a base is a good idea. A base should provide toe space of at least 3½ inches in height and 2¾ inches in depth. If you plan to mount the unit on casters, you'll automatically get toe space that makes the project convenient.

Box base. This easy-to-build recessed base consists of a four-sided open box installed at the

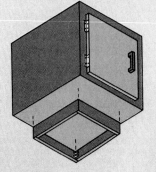

bottom of the cabinet or storage unit. Since appearance is not a factor, you can construct the box with simple butt joints and secure it to the cabinet with steel angle brackets installed along the inside of the base (see sketch).

Leg base. Four short, stubby legs also make a good base. Commercial legs come with their own mounting plate, which is screwed to the bottom of the cabinet before the leg is screwed into place (see sketch). You can also install home-built legs with hanger bolts.

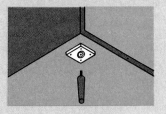

These bolts have a "wood" thread on one end and a coarse "machine" thread on the other end. Drill an undersize hole in the cabinet for the machine end, insert the hanger bolt using pliers and screw the leg into place.

A good source for low-priced legs is a lumberyard that does millwork. Quite often, they'll have a bin full of legs of all sizes that may have slight imperfections or chips which won't affect their serviceability.

How to Mount Shelves

Shelves are a quick and easy way of getting additional storage space in your home, shop, or garage. The best material for shelving is ¾-inch plywood or pine boards—8, 10, 12 inches wide, depending on the items to be stored. To prevent sagging, install a shelf support every 30 inches. And don't use hardboard or chip board, as they tend to bow under heavy loads.

STEEL SHELF BRACKET

Shelf brackets. The easiest way to mount a shelf is by means of steel shelf brackets sold in hardware stores (see sketch). Ask for brackets whose short leg is nearly equal to the *width* of the shelf you plan to install. And always mount the brackets with the *long* leg against the wall. Screw the brackets into the wall and space them about 30 inches apart. For heavy loads, shop around for brackets that have gussets connecting the two legs. Brackets without gussets tend to sway under heavy loads.

Cleats and angle brackets. The narrow space between two walls is an ideal location for shelving. Simply install a pair of cleats at the heights where you want shelves (see sketch). Use cleats that are at least ¾ inch thick and as long as the shelf is wide.

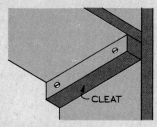

CLEAT

If the walls are of masonry, secure the cleats with so-called steel cut nails (wear goggles when driving these, as they may break off if not struck head-on). Secure the cleats with screws if the walls are of wood, or use flange bolts if they're hollow.

You can also use small steel angle brackets. Mount two under each side of the shelf as shown.

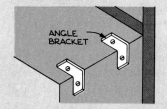

ANGLE BRACKET

Dowels. Another method of supporting shelves is with dowels. Drill holes equal to the diameter of the dowels, and bore them deep enough to accept at least ½-inch of dowel length. (Make sure both left and right holes are the same height; you might use a level on the shelves to ensure exact mounting.)

Use ¼-inch dowels for light-duty shelves and ⅜-inch dowels for shelves supporting heavy loads. Beveling the dowel ends

will make them easier to insert into the holes. To change shelf spacing, simply drill additional holes.

Dado cuts. This method of supporting shelves has long been a favorite with master cabinetmakers. First, determine the height of the shelf, mark the uprights, and make your cuts. Then cut the shelf to fit.

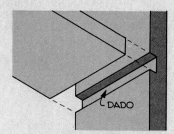

DADO

Metal tracks and brackets. You can recess or surface-mount these handy shelf supports. Shelf brackets, specially designed to fit into the track slots, are made to accept 8-, 10-, and 12-inch-wide shelves. Special brackets which adjust to hold shelves at a downward slope also are available and are used to hold dictionaries and reference books.

These tracks and brackets are available in finishes to match the decor of practically any room.

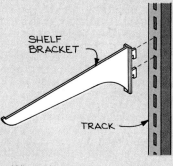

SHELF BRACKET

TRACK

When installing shelves in a cabinet, mount two tracks on each side of the cabinet and use small clips to hold the shelves in place. To change the spacing between shelves, just remove the clips and reposition.

Furring strips. These are especially useful for supporting and erecting shelves in the garage or workshop. Use 2x4s bolted or screwed to the wall and short lengths of 1x4s for shelf supports, as indicated in the drawing. Note that one end is dadoed into the 2x4 (½-inch depth is enough). The

front end of the shelf support bracket is supported by a 1x2 cut at a 45 degree angle at the bottom and engages a cutout called a *bird's mouth* at the top. Toenail

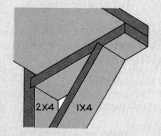

2X4   1X4

the lower end of the 1x2 into the 2x4. There's no need to nail the upper end, as the weight of the shelf will keep it in place.

Support from above. While most shelves are supported from the bottom, you can also support them from the top. This top support method is especially applicable in basement areas where the joists are exposed. You can nail 2x4s to the joists and fit any type of

project—open shelves, a cabinet, even a work surface between them. If the project to be suspended will run perpendicular to the joists, be careful to plan the length so that it will match the spacing of the joists.

Another way to support shelving from the top is use threaded rods (see sketch above). Choose rods from ¼- to ¾-inch diameter according to the load you'll support. Drill holes in the shelves slightly oversize. To attach the upper end of the rod, drill holes in 2x2 scraps and screw to the joists. Insert the rod and add a nut and washer to the top.

Then install the shelves with a nut and washer on both top and bottom. Tighten the nuts securely to give the shelves as much stability as possible.

HOW TO MAKE DRAWERS

Next to shelves, drawers are the most convenient place for storage. And a drawer is comparatively easy to build. It's just a five-sided box, connected at its corners with the joints previously described.

Types of Drawers

Drawers, no matter how they're made, fall into two general classifications—the flush or recessed type, and the lip type.

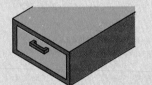

Flush drawers. You must fit this type of drawer carefully to the cabinet opening, with only enough clearance at top and sides to facilitate sliding in and out. In fact, some custom cabinetmakers often will make flush-type drawers with a taper of 1/16 inch from front to back to ensure a good appearance and an easy-sliding fit.

Lipped drawers. These drawers have an oversize front panel that completely covers the drawer opening and so offers much greater leeway in fitting the drawer into its recess.

One way to make a lipped drawer is to rabbet the front panel to the sides and bottom of the drawer, leaving an overlap of ½ inch or so. A simpler way is to screw a false front to the finished drawer front. With this method, if there is any error in construction, the false front will hide it. Attach the drawer front with countersunk flathead screws from the *inside* of the drawer. In addition to the screws, apply white glue between the two pieces.

Construction Details

When making drawers, remember to make the cabinet first, then fit the drawers to the cabinet openings. To make a drawer, first determine its length and cut two pieces of wood to this size and the required width. (The width, of course, will be the height of the finished drawer.)

Draw two parallel lines, equal to the thickness of the drawer back, about ½ inch from the ends

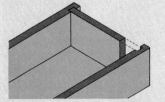

of the two pieces. Cut a dado between these lines to a depth of ¼ inch.

Next, measure the inside distance between the two sides of the drawer opening and cut the drawer back to this measurement. (Allow for clearance and the depth of the dado cuts in the drawer sides.)

For the front of the drawer, plan simple butt joints and cut it to allow a ¼-inch overhang on all sides, if you plan a lip.

You are now ready to partially assemble the drawer. Brush some white glue into the two dado cuts and install the back panel. Use three or four brads at each joint to secure the sides. Next attach the drawer front using glue and brads or screws to secure it to the sides.

A false front nailed or screwed to the existing front from the inside of the drawer will conceal the original brads or screws. If you use brads, countersink them with a nail set.

The bottom of the drawer consists of ¼-inch or thicker plywood, and is nailed to the sides and back of the drawer. For stronger, more elaborate construction, you can use any one of the woodworking joints described earlier in this section.

Drawer Runners and Guides

To ensure that the drawers you build will move in and out without wobbling, you can use any one of

three methods: guides located at each side of the drawer; a central guide placed at the bottom of the drawer; or commercial metal tracks mounted on the sides of the cabinet with nylon wheels on the drawer sides. These come in lengths to fit most drawers and are especially good for heavy loads. Select them before you build the drawer in order to plan the clearance space.

The simplest guide consists of two narrow lengths of wood secured to each side of the drawer, spaced an inch apart (see sketch). Another strip of wood, mounted on each side of the

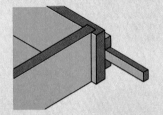

drawer opening, fits the "track" mounted on the drawer sides. To ease operation, apply paste wax to all touching surfaces.

For guides at the bottom of the drawer, mount lengths of wood on the cabinet and engage the two strips of wood on the bottom of the drawer.

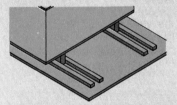

If you're planning to incorporate runners and guides in the drawers, make allowances before starting work. A clearance of ½-inch is required for guides mounted at the sides of the drawers, and 1 inch for center-mounted guides. Regardless of what type of drawer guides you use, make sure you install them accurately.

You can even make easy-sliding drawers without guides or runners by installing plastic glides in the drawer openings so the bottom of the drawer will bear against plastic instead of wood. Steel thumbtacks also ease drawer movement. But don't forget to apply wax to the bottom bearing surfaces of the drawer.

HOW TO INSTALL CABINET DOORS

Except for shelves, tables, and chairs, nearly every piece of furniture you build will have some sort of door. All doors require hinges or tracks, and handles for opening and closing. Here are the basics.

Construction Pointers

To prevent warping, cabinet doors should be at least ½ inch thick. However, you can use a ¼-inch panel, providing you frame it with ½-inch wood, somewhat like a picture frame.

If you plan to laminate a door panel with plastic, use the thin grade laminate especially made for vertical surfaces. The heavy grade, made for countertops, may cause the cabinet to warp.

Sliding Doors

Sliding doors are easier to fit and install than swinging doors, and, as a rule, are of much lighter stock than conventional doors. Track for sliding doors can be aluminum or plastic (left sketch), or it can consist of grooves cut into the top and bottom of the framework (right sketch).

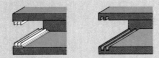

Of course, you must cut these grooves before assembly. Make the upper grooves about twice as deep as the bottom ones so you can lift up, then lower the door into place. The doors should be flush with the bottom shelf surface when it's touching the top of the upper groove.

To ease sliding, apply wax or a silicone spray to the grooves. If you're planning to use handles, recess them into the door so there will be no interference when the doors bypass each other.

Hinged Doors

Flush-type hinged doors that recess within the framing require clearance all around to prevent binding. To install a flush-type door, make a dry fit, and if the door fits, insert small wedges at all sides to hold it in place and ensure clearance until the hinges have been completely installed.

Then place the hinge against the door—if it's an exterior mounting—and mark the hinge holes with an awl. Drill pilot holes and install the hinges. Use this same procedure if you have an interior mounting job.

With hinges that are partly concealed—half on the inside of the door and half on the frame—mount the hinges on the door first, set the door in place, and mark the location of the hinge on the frame or door jamb. This method is much easier than trying to fit an already-mounted hinge to the blind or interior part of the door.

Types of hinges. There are literally dozens of types of hinges to choose from. Following are a few of the more common varieties.

As a general rule, you should mortise hinges into cabinets so they are flush with the work. However, always surface mount decorative hinges, such as colonial, rustic, and ornamental hinges.

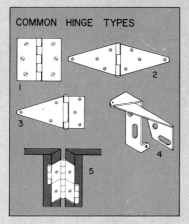

COMMON HINGE TYPES

(1) *Butt hinges* are the type you're probably most familiar with. Use them for either right- or left-hand doors. The larger sizes have removable pins to facilitate taking off the door; the smaller sizes don't. For long cabinet doors or lids. use a piano hinge (a long butt hinge) rather than several smaller ones. (2, 3) The *strap hinge* and the *T hinge* are used for extra-heavy doors. There's no need to mortise these hinges, as they are strictly functional.

(4) *Pivot hinges,* also called knife hinges, are available in different shapes and are especially good for use on ¾-inch plywood doors. All shapes present a very unobtrusive appearance.

(5) *Double-acting hinges* allow a door to be swung from either direction.

Self-closing hinges operate by means of a spring concealed within the barrel of the hinge. Another type, used on kitchen cabinets, has no spring, yet closes the door with a positive snapping action. Its secret is a square shoulder next to the pin.

Special-purpose hinges are available with offset leaves (so the door will overlap the framing); hinges with knuckles (for quick door removal); ball-bearing hinges lubricated for life (for extra-heavy doors); hinges that will automatically raise a door when it is opened (so that it will clear a carpet on the far side of the door); burglar-resistant hinges (with pins that can't be removed when they're on the outside); and hinges that allow a door to be swung back far enough so that the full width of the doorway can be utilized.

Door catches and handles. In addition to hinges, you will need hardware to keep the doors closed and to lock them. For cabinet work, your best hardware bets are spring-loaded or magnetic catches.

Spring-loaded catches come with single and double rollers and are ideal for lipped doors, flush doors, double doors, and shelves. These catches are adjustable.

Install magnetic catches so there is physical contact between the magnet in the frame and the "keeper" on the door.

A handle of some type is required for all drawers and doors. Handles can be surface-mounted or recessed flush with the drawer or door. Sliding doors always use recessed handles so the doors can bypass each other.

THE HARDWARE YOU'LL NEED

For any sort of fastening work, you will need nails, screws, and bolts, as well as glues and cements.

Nails, Screws, and Bolts

These most common of all fastening materials are available in diverse widths and lengths, and in steel, brass, aluminum, copper, and even stainless steel.

Nails. Nails are sold by the penny—which has nothing to do with their cost. The "penny," (abbreviated *d*) refers to the size. The chart shows a box nail marked in the penny size designations as well as actual lengths in inches.

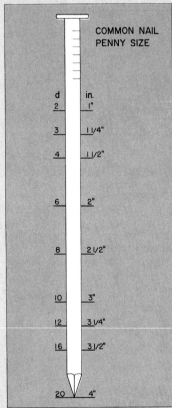

COMMON NAIL PENNY SIZE

d	in.
2	1"
3	1 1/4"
4	1 1/2"
6	2"
8	2 1/2"
10	3"
12	3 1/4"
16	3 1/2"
20	4"

Use common nails for general-purpose work; finish and casing nails for trim or cabinetwork; and brads for attaching molding to walls and furniture.

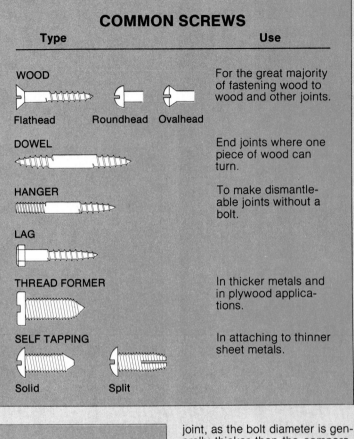

COMMON SCREWS

Type	Use
WOOD Flathead Roundhead Ovalhead	For the great majority of fastening wood to wood and other joints.
DOWEL	End joints where one piece of wood can turn.
HANGER	To make dismantleable joints without a bolt.
LAG	
THREAD FORMER	In thicker metals and in plywood applications.
SELF TAPPING Solid Split	In attaching to thinner sheet metals.

Finishing

Casing

Brad

Screws. Screws are sold by length and diameter. The diameter is indicated by a number, from 1 to 16. The thicker the screw shank, the larger the number. The drawing shows some of the most popular types of screws.

Always drill a pilot hole when inserting a screw into hardwood. And always drill a clearance hole in the leading piece of wood when screwing two pieces of wood together. Without a clearance hole, the leading piece tends to "hang up," preventing a tight fit between the two.

Bolts. You can also fasten wood together with bolts, but only if there is access to the back for the required washer and nut. A bolted joint is stronger than a screwed joint, as the bolt diameter is generally thicker than the comparable screw, and also because the wrench used to tighten the nut can apply much more force than a screwdriver in a screw slot.

Glues and Cements

While not "hardware" as such, glue is an important adjunct to any fastening job. The so-called white glue is excellent for use with wood, and only moderate clamping pressure is required. When dry, it is crystal clear. However, it's not waterproof so don't use it for work subject to excessive dampness—and of course, never for outdoor use. Use the two-tube epoxy "glue" for joints that must be waterproof.

Plastic resin glue, a powder that you mix with water to a creamy consistency, is highly water resistant.

Contact cement provides an excellent bond between wood and wood, and wood and plastic. When working with contact cement, remember that it dries instantly and position your surfaces

COMMON BOLTS

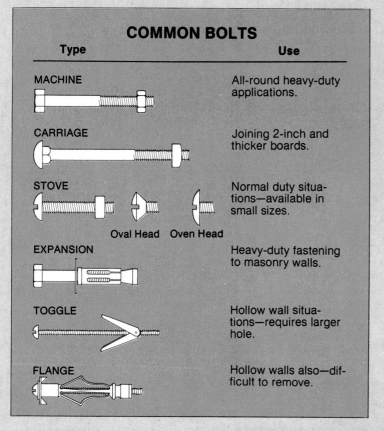

Type	Use
MACHINE	All-round heavy-duty applications.
CARRIAGE	Joining 2-inch and thicker boards.
STOVE — Oval Head, Oven Head	Normal duty situations—available in small sizes.
EXPANSION	Heavy-duty fastening to masonry walls.
TOGGLE	Hollow wall situations—requires larger hole.
FLANGE	Hollow walls also—difficult to remove.

When to Use What Glue

Type	Use
White glue (No mixing)	Paper, cloth, wood
Epoxy (requires mixing)	Wood, metal, stone (waterproof)
Plastic resin (requires mixing)	Wood to wood (water resistant)
Contact cement (no mixing)	Wood to wood or plastic (waterproof)
Waterproof glue (requires mixing)	Wood to wood (waterproof)

together exactly as you want them. You won't get a second chance.

True waterproof glue comes in two containers; one holds a liquid resin, the other a powder catalyst. When dry, this glue is absolutely waterproof and can be safely used for garden equipment and all outdoor projects and furniture.

Glides and Casters

The intended use determines whether a piece of furniture needs a caster or a glide. If you don't plan to move it frequently, use a glide; otherwise, a caster is the best choice.

Glides come in many sizes, determined by the glide area touching the floor, and with steel or plastic bottoms. The simple nail-on glides aren't height adjustable but you can adjust screw glides by screwing the glide in or out to prevent wobbling if the floor is uneven, or if by some chance, the project does not have an even base.

Casters are made in two styles—stem type (only the stem type is adjustable) and plate type (at left in sketch). The stem type requires a hole to be drilled into the leg or base of the cabinet or furniture. This hole accepts a sleeve that in turn accepts the stem of the caster.

The plate type caster is merely screwed to the bottom by four screws that pass through holes in the plate. They are not height adjustable unless, of course, you use shims.

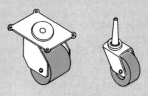

All casters use ball bearings as part of the plate assembly to facilitate swiveling. For extra-heavy usages, purchase casters with ball-bearing wheels as well.

The wheels on casters are of two types—plastic or rubber. Use casters with plastic wheels if the project is to be rolled on a soft surface such as a rug; rubber wheeled casters are best on hard concrete, vinyl, or hardwood. It's a good idea to use graphite to lubricate the wheels and their bearings, as oil tends to pick up dust and dirt.

To prevent a caster-equipped unit from rolling, get locking casters. A small lever on the outside of the wheel locks a "brake." Brakes on only two of the four casters on a unit are sufficient.

Miscellaneous Hardware

There are many types of hardware that can come in handy when you're constructing storage bins, cabinets, chests, shelves, and other projects.

Following are some you may need from time to time: corrugated fasteners connect two boards or mend splits in wood; angle irons reinforce corners; flat and T plates also reinforce work; masonry nails secure work to concrete or brick walls; steel plates with a threaded center are used for attaching legs to cabinets; screw eyes and cup hooks allow for hanging items inside storage units; and lag screw plugs made of lead or plastic secure furring strips or shelf brackets to masonry walls.

You'll be wise to stock your workshop with most of these items in a couple of sizes. That way, you won't have to make a special trip when they're needed.

FINISHING TECHNIQUES

Finishing is your final job before you can step back and admire your work. Before starting, make sure that all nails are flush or countersunk and filled, all flathead screws are flush with the surface, all cracks are filled, and all surfaces are sanded and cleaned.

Hardboard and Chip Board

If the unit you have built is made of hardboard, about the only finish you can apply to it is paint. No preparation is needed except to remove any oil or dirt. Inasmuch as hardboard is brown—the tempered type is a darker brown—you'll need to apply at least two coats of paint if you want the final finish to be a light color.

Hardboard will accept latex or alkyd paints equally well. Between coats, let dry overnight and then sand lightly.

You also can paint chip board, flake board, and particle board, but because of their slightly rougher texture you should apply a "filler" coat of shellac first, then proceed with painting.

Plywood

Because of its comparatively low cost, fir plywood is used extensively for building projects. However, the hard and soft growth patterns in the wood will show through unless a sealer is used before painting or finishing with varnish or lacquer.

After sealing, sand lightly and finish with at least two coats of paint, varnish, or lacquer. The final step for varnish or lacquer work consists of an application of paste wax applied with fine steel wool and polishing with terry cloth or any other coarse-textured cloth.

Plywood has a pronounced end grain due to its layered construction. If your project will be on display, it's best to hide the end grain, and there are several ways to do this.

A mitered joint is the obvious solution, as then the end grain is hidden within the joint. Another

solution is wood veneer tape (see sketch). This tape comes in rolls and is really walnut, oak, mahogany, or a similar wood in a very thin strip about ¾ inch wide. Either glue it or use contact cement, applying the cement to the tape and to the plywood edges. When the cement has lost its gloss, carefully align the tape and press over the plywood edge.

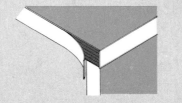

You also can use molding to cover the edges. It has the additional advantage of making a decorative edge requiring no further treatment.

Metal molding is another option, especially useful for edges which are subject to wear and abuse.

A rabbet joint will also hide end grain. Make the rabbet deep enough so that only the last ply is uncut.

Other Woods

If your project is constructed of a fine wood, a more elaborate finishing technique is needed.

Sanding. You can do this by hand or with a power sander. A power belt sander is fine for initial sanding, but always do the final sanding with an orbital or straight line finishing sander—or with fine sandpaper.

Filling and staining. Open grain woods such as oak, chestnut, walnut, ash, and mahogany require a filler to close their pores. Apply the filler with a brush or rag, wiping across the grain. After 10 or 15 minutes, remove the excess filler with a coarse cloth.

If a stain is called for, let the wood dry for 24 hours before application. A stain applied over a filler that has not dried will show up as a "hot" spot.

Sealing. A sealer, as its name implies, is used to seal the stains and filler from the subsequent finishing coats.

One of the best sealers is shellac. One advantage of using shellac is that it prevents the stain from bleeding. Thin the shellac with alcohol to the consistency of

light cream; as it comes in the can, it's much too thick for use as a sealer. You can also use ready-mixed stains combined with a sealer.

Finishes. *Varnish,* the traditional finish for wood, is available in many types and colors.

To prepare a piece for varnish, sand it lightly, wipe off the dust with a turpentine-dampened rag, and apply the varnish with long, flowing strokes. Do not brush out the varnish as you would paint. And don't use varnish during humid weather. To make sure the varnish will flow evenly, place the can in warm water.

Varnish requires at least two coats, with a minimum of 24 hours drying time. Sand lightly between coats. After the second or third coat has dried for at least a week, rub down with steel wool and paste wax. Polish with a rough cloth.

Shellac, too, will yield super results. It's fairly easy to work with and it dries dust free in a half-hour. You can apply the second coat within two hours. Sanding is not required between coats, as the second coat tends to partially dissolve and melt into the first one.

One disadvantage of shellac is that it shows a ring if a liquor-stained glass is placed on a shellac-finished surface. Also, shellac sometimes tends to crack if exposed to dampness.

Polyurethane is a tough synthetic varnish that resists abrasion, alcohol, and fruit stains. It's great for floors, furniture, walls, and woodwork. To apply polyurethane the surface must be clean, dry, and free of grease, oil, and wax. Don't apply a polyurethane finish over previously shellacked or lacquered surfaces. Allow at least 12 hours drying time for each coat, and clean your brushes with mineral spirits or turpentine.

Lacquer is a fast-drying finish you can apply by spray or brush. For spraying, thin lacquer only with lacquer thinner. *Never use turpentine or mineral spirits.*

To brush lacquer, always use a brush that has *never* been used to apply paint.

And never apply lacquer over a painted surface, as the lacquer will lift the paint. As with shellac, sanding between coats is not necessary.